The authors have very different backgrounds. **Roy Madron** spent fifteen years as a TV reporter and producer. In 1980, as a research fellow in the Participation Research Unit of the Manchester Business School, he conducted a long-term study of the use of participation strategies for improving the performance of social or business systems. He has since built on that research in his own practice as a consultant in systems improvement and participatory planning.

After practising as a barrister for thirty years, **John Jopling** has helped to establish numerous organisations seeking to contribute to a more just and healthy world. These include FIELD (Foundation for International Environmental Law and Development), Feasta (the Dublin-based foundation for the economics of sustainability) and the Sustainable London Trust, which published *Creating a Sustainable London* and *London, Pathways to the Future*. SLT is also the lead organisation in the World Wide Democracy Network, founded by the authors.

Schumacher Briefing No. 9

GAIAN DEMOCRACIES

Redefining Globalisation and People-Power

Roy Madron & John Jopling

published by Green Books
for The Schumacher Society

First published in 2003
by Green Books Ltd
Foxhole, Dartington, Totnes,
Devon TQ9 6EB
www.greenbooks.co.uk
greenbooks@gn.apc.org

for The Schumacher Society
The CREATE Centre, Smeaton Road,
Bristol BS1 6XN
www.schumacher.org.uk
admin@schumacher.org.uk

Cover design by Rick Lawrence

Printed by J.W. Arrowsmith Ltd, Bristol, UK

A catalogue record for this publication
is available from the British Library

ISBN 1 903998 28 X

Contents

Acknowledgements

It is only possible to write a work as wide-ranging and ambitious as this with a great deal of help and support. Most of the authors we have cited in the References and the Bibliography can have no idea of how valuable their work has been in shaping our thinking, and we owe them a great debt of gratitude. However, some authors and colleagues have made specific contributions that have considerably improved our original text, or given us the kind of encouragement that means so much in any creative enterprise. We would therefore like to express our warmest thanks to Gary Alexander, Phillip Allott, Luke Ashton, Brian Bloom, Bruce Buchanan, Don Chisholm, Lindsey Colbourne, Richard Douthwaite, Mark Garavan, Richard David Hames, Stephan Harding, Allen Hammond, James Lovelock, Gunter Pauli, John Raven, Phil Richardson, Samir Rihani, Allan Savory, Lloyd Timberlake and Shann Turnbull.

The unenviable task of checking references and incorporating amendments required by the authors fell to John Turnbull, our Associate at the World Wide Democracy Network. His care and attention is reflected in the final product.

As comparatively inexperienced authors, we could not have asked for a more skilled, sympathetic and challenging editor than Herbie Girardet. Moreover, it was he who commissioned the work from us on behalf of the Schumacher Society. The Gaian Democracies enterprise will always be indebted to Herbie and to the Schumacher Society for their vision and openness.

Finally, our heartfelt thanks go to our families and friends who have commented on various stages of the draft and cheered us on our sometimes tortuous and difficult path.

Roy Madron and John Jopling
February 2003

Foreword
by Dr Samir Rihani

Democracy has been roundly abused, more so now than ever before. Overt abuse is easy to see through. The most oppressive regimes often incorporate 'democratic' in their title. Only a handful of sycophants take this self-delusion seriously.

Insidious abuse practiced by states that cite 'democratic' behaviour as their distinguishing hallmark is an altogether different matter. At home, they boast of having political parties but there is little choice and the electorate have lost the incentive to vote. Abroad, they claim it as their aim in life to spread the virtues of democracy far and wide but their actions belie their words.

The claims are always lofty, and seem to follow the principle that you should tell a whopper when you mean to lie. Woodrow Wilson declared in 1917 that "the world must be made safe for democracy". Franklin D. Roosevelt added in 1940, "The USA must be the great arsenal of democracy." George W. Bush brought us up to date after the 11 September 2001 atrocities when he assured his fellow Americans that the terrorists hate the USA because it is democratic. On that basis, Iceland, with a record of democracy that goes back a thousand years, should be the natural focus for the terrorists' wrath!

Clearly, there is a long way to go to achieve the state of 'Gaian democracy' described so convincingly in this Schumacher Briefing. But a start on that trek is critically necessary at this point in time. The election that brought George W. Bush to power was a stark reminder that the 'arsenal of democracy' is in a sorry state. Somoza, the Nicaraguan dictator, was at least candid in his response when accused of ballot rigging, "You won the election, but I won the count." Bush dispensed with these niceties, and few were surprised or concerned. This resigned attitude is alarming.

Similarly, the actions of New Labour in government leave little room for anyone to accuse this administration of being overly democratic. Yet, only a few at home or abroad are prepared, at least openly, to challenge these malpractices. They are assumed to be part of the games politicians play. This cynicism is also frightening.

People feel powerless, misinformed, and disenfranchised. Civil liberties are curtailed in the 'battle against terror', and wars are waged at great expense but for obscure reasons and with little public support. At the same time, pensions are shrinking and public services are in disarray because 'the country cannot afford the cost'. Apathy and despair could spell the end of the modicum of democracy that was laboriously won over the centuries.

Foreign policies adopted by 'democratic' governments are even more worrying. The leading powers seem eager to nip democracy in the bud wherever and whenever it suits their purposes. I gave many examples of this short-sighted practice in my book on development, covering the full range from Algeria to Zaire. So-called democratic powers go further by installing, funding, and arming repressive dictators, and in some cases outright terrorists.

Democracy is not merely free speech, political parties and periodic elections. It involves all aspects of daily existence; including management, family life and, yes, politics. Sustained and healthy progress towards social, political and economic stability and development can only be made if all members of the community are both able and free to take part and be engaged at all levels and at all times. There are sound technical reasons why this is so, mainly to do with the fact that nations function as complex adaptive systems rather than as simple mechanistic entities.

The authors of this Briefing use 'soft-systems theory' to describe convincingly a plausible form of government, based on Gaian democracies, that would yield better results than the current inadequate model of 'democracy'. The transformation is not put forward simply as a desirable add-on or an optional extra. Roy Madron and John Jopling argue with passion and conviction that a radical shift is the key to harmony, stability, and sustainable evolution. Fundamentally, they demonstrate that it is not enough to 'modernise', 're-engineer', or 'reform' this or that sector of our life, such as education or health. We have to review and update our understanding and practice of democracy in the first instance. This is the challenge thrown down by this Briefing. For our sake, and that of coming generations, let us hope the challenge is picked up.

Dr Samir Rihani is a Senior Research Fellow at the School of Politics, University of Liverpool and author of *Complex Systems Theory and Development Practice*, ZED Books, 2002

Summary and Introduction

Redefining globalisation and people-power

In the midst of the prosperity and affluence of Western 'democracies' there is a pervasive sadness and sense of impotence about the future of our societies, of humanity and of the natural world. Many well-informed people have focused those negative feelings on the idea of 'globalisation'. For them the very term carries with it a sense of global despoliation, greed, oppression, injustice and irreparable loss. At the same time, many of us in the West are uncomfortably aware that the unprecedented material abundance we enjoy is being bought at the expense of the rest of the world's peoples, natural resources and wildlife. Within the societies forced to pay the costs of today's form of globalisation, tens of millions of citizens are seething with anger, envy and frustration.

Yet today's globalisation is but the latest—and hopefully temporary—phase of a globalising process that has been going on for thousands of years. In effect, we humans are a global species: we have evolved the capacity to inhabit virtually every corner of the planet. Thus some form of 'globalisation' is part of our destiny. What is in question is the form that human globalisation will take in its next manifestation.

Like millions of people, we have come to the conclusion that today's globalisation is fundamentally unjust and unsustainable. Like them we want to make a useful contribution to changing this unjust and unsustainable system of globalisation into a just and sustainable one. But we believe that to bring about such a fundamental change in an enormous and complex system we first have to understand its main characteristics **as a system**. Thus in Chapter 1 we introduce some of the key concepts and insights from systems theory, in particular 'soft-systems theory', as the basic grammar of 'a new language of change'. Soft-systems theory is the branch of systems science that deals with human systems.

In Chapter 2 we apply those concepts to a review of the environmental, social and economic impacts of today's form of globalisation on the world's peoples, natural resources and wildlife. We cite sources and material in Chapter 2 that will be familiar to many readers. However, by adopting the systems concepts and insights from Chapter 1, we are able to shed new light on what might otherwise be a rather familiar recital of the ills that globalisation has produced.

In Chapter 3, by again using a systems approach, we can see that the huge range of unjust and unsustainable impacts we describe in Chapter 2 is not haphazard. **The unjust and unsustainable aspects of globalisation stem from the purposes, principles and ideologies of a purposeful human system we have called the 'Global Monetocracy'.** In systems terms, injustice and unsustainability are 'emergent properties' of the system a whole. As a purposeful human system, the Global Monetocracy is not designed to deliver justice and sustainability. For this reason, we do not attach blame to any specific group or class. Many people, not just the financial and business elites, have prospered immensely in the service of the Global Monetocracy. There are others who defend it ferociously against its many critics. Even so, they are just minor components of a complex system that has evolved over several centuries. To blame them as individuals, or specific groups or classes, is to make a fundamental strategic error. If we want a just and sustainable global system in the future, it is the Global Monetocracy as a whole that must be reconfigured—the totality, not just parts of it.

Our description of today's global system as the Global Monetocracy originates from our identification of its core purpose **as a system**. Every human system has a purpose that governs the way it works, and this is true of today's form of globalisation. The systemic purpose of the Global Monetocracy is **the continuation of money growth in order to maintain the current debt-based money-system**. It is not widely known that almost all the money we use comes into existence, not by governments creating it, but as a result of a bank agreeing to make a loan to a customer at interest. Only about 3%—the notes and coins—is government-made. The other 97% comes into existence as a debt owed by a customer to a bank. We cite authorities such as James Robertson, Richard Douthwaite and

Michael Rowbotham to show that the effect of this is that our economies **have to grow in order to avoid financial collapse**. The debt-money system is thus the driving force behind the Global Monetocracy. The risk of collapse forces governments to give priority to policies that serve the money growth imperative; and in turn, these policies produce the unjust and unsustainable form of globalisation that we have today.

The blatant injustice and unsustainability of the Global Monetocracy has already aroused a great deal of opposition. In Chapter 4 we briefly summarise the limitations of the strategies employed by its leading opponents.

In Chapter 5 we outline the components of 'Gaian Democracy', a model of government that we believe will ensure our societies can use systems concepts to become—and remain—just and sustainable.

'Gaia' is the name of the Greek goddess of Earth. James Lovelock adopted it for the scientific theory he first put forward in 1972, in the journal *Atmospheric Environment*. The Gaia theory sees the planet's physical, chemical and biological systems as a single evolving, self-regulating ecosystem. It explores how these systems interact to maintain the overall temperature and the chemical composition of the land, the atmosphere and the sea, within limits that make the Earth habitable by countless billions of living creatures. This way of thinking about the planet—thinking within the framework of Gaia theory—has led to many important new perceptions in the sciences of the Earth, and has contributed to the foundation of a new, multi-disciplinary effort known as Earth System Science.[1]

Gaia's systems are all self-organising and interactive. We have called the form of government we are proposing Gaian Democracy, because our proposal is shaped by principles similar to those of the Gaian system itself.

Our proposal is also, crucially, based on the insights from soft-systems thinking that are outlined in Chapter 1. Gaian systems have evolved naturally. If we are to purposefully and consciously reconfigure our democratic and economic systems, we need to make use of the most soundly based and well-tried strategies for bringing about change in human societies. These are to be found in soft-systems thinking.

In Chapter 6 we discuss some of the factors that encourage us to believe that a vision of a global network of just and sustainable Gaian democracies is not a pipe-dream, but is in fact highly practical and entirely feasible.

In short, this Briefing argues that, since today's Global Monetocracy has been devised to serve an unjust and unsustainable set of purposes, we need to replace it with a global network of just and sustainable Gaian democracies.

Taking on the power of the Global Monetocracy

The elites of the Global Monetocracy use many varieties of power to influence the actions of hundreds of millions of people every minute of every day in every part of the planet. They have always been ready to use the most unscrupulous and brutal methods to enforce their aims and to defend their privileges. But these are just the tip of a vast apparatus of power. Power does not only flow from the barrel of a gun, a tear-gas canister or the use of the torture chamber by surrogates of the system. With great skill and determination, the Global Monetocracy's elites use the power of property, personality, tradition, technology, myth, propaganda, the media, government, professional and technical expertise, the judiciary and the police, patronage and, crucially, the power of ideology.

If today's unjust and unsustainable Global Monetocracy is to be replaced by a global network of just and sustainable Gaian democracies, the question of 'power' must be addressed. What alternative forms of power could be generated to bring about a fundamental global transformation in the face of the huge variety of power that the Global Monetocracy can command? To answer that question we have to understand the difference between change strategies and defence strategies.

Change strategies and defence strategies

To illustrate the vital difference between 'social defence' and 'social change',[2] George Lakey, the veteran American community activist, cites the rapid disillusionment of young Russians in the aftermath of their defeat of the attempted Communist coup in 1991.

Thousands of idealistic young men and women had put their

lives on the line to resist the attempted overthrow of Gorbachev's reforming government by former Soviet apparatchiks. Yet even though they had stopped the communist old guard in its tracks and put Yeltsin into power, they soon saw him and his ministers helping the rich to get even richer and driving the poor ever deeper into poverty. By the time Lakey encountered them a few years later, the young Russians were psychologically devastated by the aftermath of their courageous resistance to a return to totalitarianism. They were finding it extremely painful to have to face the fact that they—or as they saw themselves, 'the people of Russia'—had "lost their big move for radical change".

With his many years of experience in the black community's protest and resistance movements, Lakey was able to point out that what they had been doing in the streets of Moscow was a hugely courageous example of social **defence** of their society, but that the kind of social **change** they ultimately wanted to achieve would take a lot more than idealism and raw courage. "A strategy for fundamental change is a quite different project from what the pro-democracy Russians did, which was to defend Gorbachev and what he represented (the status quo) against the attack by the reactionaries."

Lakey's social defence vs social change dialectic opened the eyes of the young Russians. They now realised that to achieve the kind of change they wanted for the Russian people called for a strategy for change. This would entail bringing together the popular movements—who were concerned with defending the things they valued—around a vision of what a genuinely democratic Russia would look like. Upon that shared vision they would then be able to build a viable **political** movement to campaign at elections for every office in the land.

As this Briefing explains, we need to replace today's unjust and unsustainable Global Monetocracy with a global network of just and sustainable Gaian democracies. Consequently, as George Lakey makes clear, if such hugely ambitious changes are to happen we must set about building **viable political movements** to offer the vision of Gaian democracies to people in every country where elections are held.

The Gaian model of democracy is shaped by the conviction that, with the tools provided by soft-systems methodologies, the peoples of the world have the political capacities to co-create global networks of just and sustainable Gaian democracies. As we explain in Chapter 5, the fundamental political and governmental changes we need cannot be initiated and sustained without at first thousands, and ultimately millions of active citizens thinking, acting and learning together to co-create societies that are just and sustainable. We agree with Professor David Held, when he says, "Our established ideas about equality, justice and liberty [and, we would say, sustainability] have to be refashioned into a coherent political project robust enough for a world where power is exercised not just locally and nationally but also on a trans-national scale, and where the consequences of political and economic decisions in one community can ramify across the globe."[3]

By its very nature, the Gaian democracies project must be capable of handling and tackling effectively a tremendous variety of issues, while building and sustaining the trust and commitment of the citizens it seeks to serve. If future historians are to judge today's Global Monetocracy to have been a painful but temporary cul-de-sac, the Gaian democracies project will have to cross all boundaries and include all disciplines. It will need to have many starting points in order to build the necessary power and range of competencies needed to fulfil its purpose. Those starting points will most likely arise at the margins of the Global Monetocracy's empire. No matter how small and how tentative those initial steps may be, the Gaian democracies project will gain in strength and certainty through citizens sharing their experiences of thinking, acting and learning together to bring about fundamental social, economic and political change. When citizens think, act and learn together they build the shared competencies and understanding through which effective forms of people-power can be generated.

With an accelerating accumulation of shared experiences, competencies and people-power, there will eventually be a tipping point at which 'globalisation' will come to mean the global network of Gaian democracies, rather than the Global Monetocracy. By that point the vast varieties of power that the elites of the Global Monetocracy have at their command will have evaporated. Instead, the global network of Gaian democracies will be exercising a very different but equally comprehensive variety of powers to serve a very different range of purposes.

The sooner that tipping point is reached, the better it will be. As we explain in Chapter 2, if it is delayed much beyond thirty years the environmental and social consequences could be disastrous for the human family and many other species. But in order to reach the tipping point as soon as possible the Gaian democracies political project will need to learn from all the practical examples of people-power from which we have drawn much of the material for Chapter 5.

People-power in the real world

As the diagram at the beginning of Chapter 5 shows, the key components of Gaian democracies are:

- The Gaian system

- Shared purposes and principles

- Soft-systems concepts

- Paulo Freire's learning principles

- Participatory change processes

- Liberating political leadership

- Network government

Together these seven components provide the systemic basis of Gaian democracies, enabling them to generate the people-power that will re-define 'globalisation' in terms of a network of just and sustainable societies. To illustrate some of the concepts on which we have based our thinking we have chosen the following examples of organisations and governments, which have adopted and applied several of the components of Gaian Democracy. In so doing, the forms of people-power they have generated have led them to reconfigure their enterprises and achieve outstanding success. In the space available, we can give only a brief sketch of each example, but fuller accounts are available at *www.wwdemocracy.org*.

The success of these examples, in highly competitive environments, can be attributed to their development of structures and processes whose complexity matches that of the environments they have to contend with. As Shann Turnbull says:

"The challenge for developing *a new way to govern* is to determine the simple basic design rules to create organisations [or as we would say, Gaian democracies] that manage complexity along the same principles evolved in nature. The reason for following the rules of nature to construct ecological organisations is that these rules have proved to be the most efficient and robust way to create and manage complexity."[4] [original emphasis]

1. Examples from business

The Mondragón Corporacion Cooperativa (MCC)

Mondragón is a city in the Basque region of Spain. By the early 1990s, the cooperatives that make up the MCC had annual sales of over £4 billion. Their 53,000 worker/owners were organised in a self-governing network of firms, kept mostly to a human scale of around 500 people. When a member-cooperative grew to about 500 worker/owners, part of it was spun off into a separate business. Thus for many years the MCC grew organically, by cell division, not by take-overs or by unlimited growth in its component parts. Eventually each self-governing cooperative was part of a complex system of self-governance comprising over 1000 'compound' boards or control centres. Contrary to the received wisdom of the Global Monetocracy's elites, it was this highly complex and devolved system of governance that enabled the MCC to achieve its high levels of productivity and profitability, its stability of employment and its capacity for innovation and flexibility.

Like most of the examples we give, the MCC had 'hard-wired' its capacity to generate extraordinary levels of people-power by making very conscious decisions about its financing, organisational structure and governance processes at a very early stage of its development. The guiding spirit behind these decisions was José Maria Arrizmendi-Arrieta, a Jesuit priest who encouraged his parishioners to set up their first cooperative enterprises back in the 1940s.

Visa International

The constitution of credit card company Visa International was designed through the 'chaordic design process' invented by Dee Hock, who became its first Chief Executive. We quote Hock's insistence on the vital importance of purpose and principles in Chapter 1 and discuss them at length in Chapter 5. Once commonly understood statements of purpose and principles have been arrived at by all relevant and affected parties, it is comparatively easy to agree a constitution.

Chaordic design combines elements of competition (chaos) with elements of cooperation (order). The parties involved in setting up Visa had to decide in what respects they needed to cooperate, and in what areas they could compete. The outcome was an institution owned by its functioning parts. The 23,000 financial institutions which now create Visa's products are at the same time its owners and customers. It has multiple boards of directors, none of which can be considered superior or inferior, as each has irrevocable authority and autonomy over geographic or functional areas.

The whole subject of stakeholder ownership of corporate bodies is closely linked to Gaian Democracy. The principle is the same: people-ownership instead of money-ownership. The record shows that—provided at least some of the components of Gaian democracies are in place—it works.[5]

The Semco Corporation: São Paulo, Brazil
Like Visa's Dee Hock, Ricardo Semler is a liberating leader who emerged from the corporate world. In his best-selling book *Maverick!*, Semler describes how he used his position as owner and chief executive to transform the decision-making processes and culture of his family company, Semco:[6]

"My role is that of a catalyst. I try to create an environment in which others make decisions. Success means not making them myself."

"We have absolute trust in our employees. We offer them the chance to be partners in our business, to be autonomous and responsible."

"We are thrilled that our workers are self governing and self managing. It means that they care about their jobs and that's good for all of us."

"We get out of the way and let them do their jobs."

Specific changes included the following:

- All financial information was made freely available and open to discussion, and people were taught the skills they needed to make use of this information.

- Structures were set up to enable as many decisions as possible to be taken by the people who would implement them—circles instead of a pyramid.

- Menial jobs were shared; perks, privileges and unnecessary formality done away with.

- People were encouraged to think for themselves and use common sense.

- Fewer bosses, fewer bureaucrats. Semler himself, instead of being chief executive, became one of five 'counselors'.

Semler sees this as merely a beginning: "We have been ripping apart Semco and putting it back together again for a dozen years and we're just 30% finished." He is a tireless learner, driven by a belief in unfettered democracy, but he does not underestimate the difficulties: "Participation is infinitely more complex to practise than conventional corporate unilateralism. . . . Nothing is harder work than democracy."

2. Examples from politics

The real life democratic innovations of the greatest significance for Gaian democracies are those introduced in Athens in the 5th century BC and in Brazil since 1989.

Athens: Kleisthenes, the inventor of 'people-power'

Two and a half millennia before Semler, Kleisthenes also came from the ruling class. On becoming chief archon (mayor) of Athens in 507/8 BC, he determined to break away from the tradition of government by a small ruling elite. He seems to have asked himself: "How can I enable the 40,000 citizens of Athens to govern themselves so that together we can successfully manage the conflicting interests and demands facing us?" It is the kind of question liberating leaders ask, and Kleisthenes' answer was, "People-power!" By committing his government to people-power, Kleisthenes started the process through which Athens became the nearest thing to a genuine democracy the world has ever seen.

Like almost all societies until well into the 20th century, the Athens of 2,500 years ago excluded women (and slaves) from government, so this form of people-power was restricted to males over the age of 18. Obviously a modern Kleisthenes would not have to work within those restrictions, but, in systems terms, these historical factors do not diminish the importance of Athenian democracy as the prime example of a system of government based on people-power.

Recognising that elections favoured the well-born, the prominent and the wealthy, Kleisthenes started by re-structuring the political geography of the city, creating ten phylai (brotherhoods) of 4,000 citizens, each representing a cross-section of Athenian (male) society, so that no one class could dominate. The business of the citizens' Assembly was managed by the Boule (council). Each month fifty citizens were **chosen by lot** from one of the phylai to constitute the Boule, so that in any one year the Boule was rotated between all the phylai.

Government decisions, including the conduct of wars, were taken by the Assembly itself, meeting up to 40 times a year on the Pnyx, a large theatre-like meeting place on the hill west of the Acropolis. A quorum of 6000 was required. As John Dunn has written: "for the most part, ancient Greek citizens had far greater direct experience of politics than all but a handful of citizens in modern states. Every citizen of Athens was entitled to attend, vote and speak at meetings of the Assembly, which decided the great issues of state: the making of peace or war, the passing of laws and the political exile or death of individual leaders; and they did so by simple majorities."[7]

Professor Dunn argues that the benefits of people-power were enormous: "Kleisthenes turned a motley, insecure and essentially powerless aggregation of residents in a vaguely demarcated territory into a proud and self-confident sovereign people." Seventy years after Kleisthenes' death, the legendary soldier and statesman, Pericles, summarised Athenian Democracy thus: ". . . the city of Athens, taken all together, is a model for all Greece, and each Athenian, as far as I can see, is more self-reliant as an individual and behaves with exceptional versatility and grace in the more varied forms of activity."

It is no coincidence that it was during this period, while it was engaged in the world's first experiment in people-power, that the city of Athens saw the flowering of one of the most humane, adventurous, artistic and influential civilisations there has ever been.

The 'Orçamento Participativo' or Participatory Budget Process

The benefits of people-power are being experienced today in over 100 Brazilian cities, and especially by the 1.3 million residents of Porto Alegre, the capital of Brazil's southernmost state, Rio Grande do Sul. It was in Porto Alegre that the Participatory Budget (PB) process was first attempted. Since 1989, Porto Alegre has been governed by a left-wing coalition led by the Brazilian Workers' Party (PT). In a whole range of sectors—housing, public transport, highways, garbage collection, clinics, hospitals, sewerage, environment, literacy, schooling, culture, law and order—the city has made spectacular progress. The key to this success has been its PB, first introduced by the PT the year after Olívio Dutra's victory in the 1988 Mayoral elections.[8]

For the purposes of the PB, the city is divided into sixteen administrative areas or regions. To enable an integrated vision for the whole of the city to be defined, there are five citywide themes: public transport and traffic; education; culture and leisure; healthcare and social security; economic development and taxation; and city management and urban development.

The PB process takes nine months, starting in April. The first round assemblies—in all of which the Mayor participates—are held in each of the sixteen regions and on the five themes. These review the basic components of the budget and major investments of the previous year. Then neighbourhood and sub-thematic meetings are held to identify investment priorities. The second round assemblies take place in June, when investment proposals are presented to the city's senior officials.

Each region has an elected Regional Budget Forum that coordinates neighbourhood priorities into a list of priorities for the region as a whole. The Forum then settles any disputes with the various city agencies, and negotiates and monitors the implementation by those agencies. The elected Municipal Budget Council coordinates the demands made in each of the regional and thematic forums in order to produce the city's annual investment plan.

In addition to the improvement in municipal services, the PB has greatly reduced corruption while increasing the incidence of neighbourhood mobilisation and active citizenship. Poorer people in particular find it a more effective way to exercise their rights and responsibilities of citizenship than voting at elections. In 2002 over 45,000 citizens and 1000 local organisations and enterprises participated in Porto Alegre's PB.

People-power and liberating leadership

Each of the above examples shows some of the components of Gaian Democracy at work in the real world. They are by no means templates for Gaian democracies: women and slaves were excluded from public life in Athens; Semco, Visa and Mondragón all operate within the Global Monetocracy. However, in every case they illustrate the need for liberating leadership, whether in the corporate world—as with Dee Hock, Ricardo Semler or José Maria Arrizmendi-Arrieta—or in the political world—as shown by Kleisthenes and Pericles in Athens and the Workers' Party in Brazil. They show that people-power is immensely rewarding for all the people concerned and for the system as a whole. They suggest the wide diversity of situations in which the model could be applied. And they all show that the kinds of changes involved in creating Gaian democracies can be peacefully initiated and sustained by liberating leaders who are prepared to 'hard-wire' people-power into the principles, purposes, structure, organisation and processes of their enterprise.

None of our examples illustrates a society that has succeeded in reforming its economy so as to become just and sustainable. There are of course thousands of projects and initiatives around the world which have these aims and which the Gaian democracies of the future can build on. But, as no society can insulate itself from the Global Monetocracy, there are no examples of modern societies co-existing in a symbiotic relationship with the rest of the Gaian systems. Hence the need to reconfigure the Global Monetocracy itself.

The transition phase

In every one of the examples we have cited above, the fundamental changes were initiated in the most unpromising circumstances. The people of Mondragón had been devastated by Franco's victory in the Spanish Civil War and were suffering harsh repression. Dee Hock and a small team worked out the enormously radical organisational concepts that eventually became the trillion dollar Visa International at a time when conventional credit card businesses were losing hundreds of millions of dollars a year in the USA. Semco was lurching from crisis to crisis and heading towards bankruptcy when Ricardo Semler converted himself from a command-and-control workaholic to a laid-back liberating leader: then he could start the process by which the people in the company were empowered to turn it into a huge success. In the decade before Kleisthenes became archon of Athens, the city had been ruined by a violently autocratic tyrant, and suffered the indignity of being policed by 'advisers' from Sparta and governed by puppets of the Spartan regime.

When Olívio Dutra was elected mayor of Porto Alegre he inherited a shambles that was getting worse by the day: the city had been bankrupted by the previous Mayor and his party; there were virtually no public services in the poorest parts of the city; and corruption was endemic at every level in the administration. Then, as now, the PT's political opponents controlled the local newspapers, radio stations and TV channels. The growing electoral success of the Brazilian PT is therefore especially encouraging for political parties engaged in uphill struggles to build people-powered Gaian democracies elsewhere in the world. In each election in Porto Alegre since 1988, the PT has been rewarded for its liberating leadership by an increased percentage of the vote. In the 2000 mayoral elections the PT candidate was supported by more than 63% of the electorate. And, most encouraging of all, the PT's Lula da Silva won 61% of the national vote in the 2002 presidential elections.

The leaders of these enterprises knew that the old ways had turned out to be a recipe for certain disaster. In each case their new ideas involved rethinking the purposes and principles, the structures, the processes and the governance of the enterprise, whether it was an organisation or government. And at the core of these examples was a fundamental commitment by liberating leaders to people-power as the means by which disaster could be surmounted and a new way of life developed.

Moreover, each of these liberating leaders was working in virtual isolation and faced fierce opposition. Athenian people-power had to overcome the implacable hostility of the Spartan war-machine and a permanent fifth column within the Athenian elite. Porto Alegre had no other city to call on for help and guidance as it painfully learnt how to turn its commitment to people-power into a successful Participatory Budget process. Moreover, even though over 100 Brazilian cities now have PT administrations committed to people-power and participative budgets, their leaders still have to put their lives on the line. Its officials and their families routinely receive death threats, and within the last two years, two of the PT's city mayors have been assassinated. No-one had ever devised 'a chaordic organisation' before Dee Hock and his small team of middle-ranking bank officers worked it out from first principles, and then implemented it while the rest of the banking world waited for them to fail. Similar stories can be told of Semco and Mondragón.

So, starting in the most unpromising and even dangerous circumstances is the norm for liberating leaders who commit themselves to people-powered, fundamental change. People-power is sometimes hard-wired into the enterprise from its very foundation, as with Visa and Mondragón. Alternatively, and more usually, people-power can be introduced as the key element in a radical strategy for fundamental change in a crisis situation, as with Semco, Porto Alegre and Athens. These conclusions imply an almost infinite range of opportunities to introduce the Gaian Democracy model and initiate fundamental long-term change. There must be a few potential José Maria Arrizmendi-Arrietas, Dee Hocks, Ricardo Semlers, Kleisthenes and Olivio Dutros in every community, city, company, public service and political party.

There is no space in this very condensed Briefing to describe all the examples of people-powered fundamental change that we know about. What they all have in common is the application of at least some of the components that we believe are essential if Gaian democracies are to be successful. By their very nature, these examples help to move the transition process towards the tipping point when a global network of just and sustainable Gaian democracies emerges out of the unjust and unsustainable shambles of the Global Monetocracy. The Gaian Democracy political project will have to identify, encourage, support and connect all people-power change initiatives so that we can reach the tipping point as soon as possible. The longer it takes, the greater the damage that the Global Monetocracy will do to the human family and to the natural world on which we all depend.

"Real success can only come if there is a change in our societies, and in our economics, and in our politics. " —Sir David Attenborough in *The Ecologist*, April 2001.

Chapter 1

A New Language of Change

"I can't understand why people are frightened of new ideas. I'm frightened of the old ones."—John Cage (1912–1992), American philosopher, composer, poet, essayist, painter, pianist.

In every field of human endeavour, a major new development brings with it a new language. Think of how necessary it is for everyone who uses a computer to learn the meaning of words like 'hardware' and 'software', 'spreadsheet', 'database' and 'mouse'. It is virtually impossible to discuss our work with computers and the problems we have with them without using such terms. In this Briefing we are anticipating a radical new development in the world of government, politics and business. This will involve fundamentally different ways of thinking about democracy and politics, and the relationships between the human and the natural worlds. In order to discuss this we have to introduce quite a large number of concepts and terms that will be unfamiliar to most readers. However, just as those of us who had never heard the word 'cursor' or 'spreadsheet' a few years ago could not imagine working without them today, we expect such terms as 'soft-systems thinking' and 'liberating leaders' to be part of the everyday language of active citizens in a few years' time.

The reason we are introducing you to a new language of change as the basis for thinking in a radically different way about democracy and politics is that the existing language and way of thinking have led us down a cul-de-sac. The existing language of change does not help us to find a path that is radically different to that down which the Global Monetocracy is taking us. The need for profound and radical change is urgent and vital. To bring that about, **we have to start thinking, acting and learning in systems terms.**

By grasping the few basic principles of systems thinking that are outlined in this chapter, we can begin to think about what has to be changed and how to change it in a new and much more positive way. The main barrier to adopting a systems approach is not the difficulty of the concepts but our own habits of mind. Once those old habits of mind have been overcome, systems thinking helps us to see the relationships between many things we are already aware of but had previously thought about separately. Far from making everything more complicated, it often makes it simpler—certainly more comprehensible.

A glance at a newspaper shows that the list of apparently intractable social, economic and environmental problems is a long one. When we describe or think about the problems facing us we tend, whether by accident or design, to concentrate on particular so-called 'single issues': the arms trade; pollution; the loss of biodiversity; global warming; population growth; poverty; human rights abuses; unsustainable cities; terrorism; drugs; lack of food safety and so on. If we are sufficiently concerned, we will become well informed in a particular area of interest, perhaps expert on certain aspects of it. We throw enormous energy, enthusiasm, courage and commitment into our efforts to right this particular wrong or to make this bit of the world a better place. At the same time, the better informed we become, the more we sense there is a deeper problem and that the issues that particularly concern us are but symptoms of a wider malaise.

We might even say, "It is the whole system that is at fault," but without a systems language we are not able to think seriously about what we mean by 'the whole system'. Instead we fall back on terms such as 'capitalism' or 'globalisation'. While these terms provide a focus for various economic, environmental and social movements to mobilise defensive organisations, campaigns and protests, they do not lead to a purposeful strategy for change. When, in spite of their best efforts, 'the whole system' rapidly becomes even more unjust and unsustainable, its opponents and victims are left with a sense of powerlessness. The tendency to become either resigned and apathetic or angry and violent then seems fully justified, no matter how unhelpful such responses may be.

What is needed is an alternative view of the future that is not only practical and realistic in political and economic terms, but also moral and ecological. To encompass all of those requirements, the alternative cannot be a simple one. It has to be as complex as the system that it seeks to dismantle and replace. Once we begin thinking in systems terms, we will see how we can handle the moral, ecological and political dimensions of the task of making a better world.

Some basic systems concepts

We start with the conceptual dimensions of the task, introducing many of the concepts associated with systems thinking and, in particular, soft-systems thinking. Over the past fifty years, systems thinkers have become increasingly influential in every field of human endeavour—from astronomy to agriculture, from economics to health, from crime-prevention to traffic circulation. The practical benefits of systems thinking in making all sorts of systems—technical, financial, educational and health for example—work better and more humanely have been immense.[9] It is surprising how little use has been made of it in tackling the huge agenda of social and political problems that we face.[10]

However, this chapter is merely an introduction to a way of thinking about the world and organisations that has emerged over the past fifty years. In that time thousands of people have contributed to the theory and practice of systems science. They have written dozens of books to explain the many different ways in which systems concepts can be applied to help us understand how every kind of human organisation, community, society and situation can be improved and made more just and viable. An essential part of the process of understanding systems concepts is to try to apply them in particular situations and then evaluate the success of the application as a basis for doing better next time. It is in that spirit, as a basis for purposeful active learning, that this chapter has been written.

Systems science identifies three broad types of systems. None is superior to the others; each is equally valid. Their differences stem from the different contexts in which they are found, the different ways in which they have evolved and the different things that they are intended to do.

Engineered, or designed, systems

We are all familiar with engineered, or designed, systems. Cars, watches, rockets, gas supplies and computers are all engineered systems. They are what they are and they do what they do because they have been designed and built by specialists in those particular systems. Our current societies understand the nature of these systems very well. The trouble is that our world is so swamped by them that they dominate our thinking, and we tend to assume that they are the only kind of system that matters, whereas in truth the next two kinds of system are far more important for our future.

Natural systems

These include every living being, and also stable combinations of living beings. Trees, humans, snakes, bacteria and birds are natural systems. They have all evolved over millions of years to become what they are today. They have not been designed and built by specialists. Forests and coral reefs are collective natural ecosystems: they constantly change and adapt and re-generate themselves, yet they are still a forest or a coral reef.

Unlike engineered systems, living systems are not merely complicated—they are **complex**. In systems science the term 'complex' means that the way in which the system works cannot be explained purely in terms of cause and effect. There will of course be many relationships of cause and effect within the system, but the behaviour of the system **as a whole** cannot be explained in these terms. Biology, the science seeking to understand the processes of life, developed methods very different to those of chemistry and physics. As a chemist you can analyse a dead organism into its constituent chemicals and a living one in terms of its inputs and outputs. As a physicist you can measure its energy consumption or mechanical efficiency. But you cannot make sense of living organisms by reducing them to chemical components and physical attributes. A more holistic approach is needed, dealing with complexity by increasing the level of abstraction, i.e. looking at the bigger picture rather than seeking to divide the whole organism or ecosystem into manageable but separate elements.

Purposeful human 'soft' systems

Purposeful human systems, otherwise known as 'soft systems', include all of our institutions and organisations: tribes, schools, banks, armies, governments, corporations, theatre groups, orchestras, non-governmental organisations, police forces and thousands more besides. Even a casual glance will show that purposeful human systems have much in common with natural systems. They evolve, they can replicate themselves, they adapt, they can die, they are complex.

Purposeful human systems also have many things in common with engineered systems. Whether their members are aware of it or not, most of them have been (more or less) consciously configured by their dominant elites, often over many generations. They are intended to perform at least a minimum set of specific functions. In some purposeful human systems, the 'purpose' is clearly expressed and pursued by the people within the system. In most purposeful human systems, the purpose is at best vague, often disputed, rarely thought about, and still less articulated. In other purposeful human systems the purpose is deliberately said to be one thing while it is actually another. Whatever the current position, it is impossible to reconfigure purposeful human systems without first identifying, understanding and describing their current purpose and underlying values, and then working out what the different purpose and values of the reconfigured system should be. Purpose is an issue we will return to in Chapters 3 and 5.

Emergent properties

If systems are separated into their component parts they cannot perform the functions of which they are capable when put together in the right combination: a pile of bicycle parts cannot be ridden until assembled in the correct way; a tree here, some ants over there and a pile of leaves do not provide an environment in which an ecosystem can be sustained; an amputated arm cannot throw a ball. A rideable bike, ecosystems and ball throwing are 'emergent properties' of different kinds of systems. Emergent properties are the single most important concept in systems sciences because they require us to think in terms of whole systems and their relationships, not just their parts. This is what we will be seeking to do throughout this Briefing.

Self-organising

Living organisms and ecosystems are 'self-organising'. This means that their behaviour is not controlled by some external agency but is established by the system itself. Yet, even without external controls, natural systems exhibit high degrees of order. This is a consequence of the ordered but dynamic relationships between the parts of the system and its environment—between, for example, an ecosystem such as a forest and its inanimate environment.

Like living systems, purposeful human systems are also self-organising. The more complex these systems become, the more they self-organise and arrive at their own form of order, though the form of order they arrive at may or may not be helpful in achieving the system's purpose. Think of how any complex organisation you have been involved with—a local council, a hospital or a school—seems to defy all attempts to impose tight control upon it.

Adaptive

The ability of living systems and purposeful human systems to self-organise enables them to adapt to changes in their environment without losing their integrity. An ongoing enterprise is still 'the firm' after all the original staff have left and it no longer makes what it used to make. If you looked at its parts, they would all be different, but the system as a whole has retained its identity. Living and purposeful systems only 'die' when the changes in their internal or external environments are so great that they can no longer adapt to them. For example, some businesses go under when their market collapses; others manage somehow to adapt to changed conditions. Depending on the system, the fatal changes may be biological or technical, economic or political.

As we shall see in Chapter 2, the Gaian system is constantly encountering a huge range of such changes and always manages to adapt. All Gaia's subsystems have become what they are by adaptation—the process of evolution. But the rate of extinction of species is now very high due to human impact. The human species itself is currently encountering a huge range of changes, to which it may or may not be able to adapt.

We shall see in Chapter 3 how the Global Monetocracy, as a purposeful human system, has been continually adapting in order to survive. But we will also see that the challenges now facing it are so great that it cannot survive much longer. From the point of view of the human family, as another purposeful system, the process of replacing the Global Monetocracy with thousands of Gaian democracies will be a case of successful adaptation.

"The global economy is a complex adaptive system."—Professor John H. Holland of the University of Michigan.

Some features of complex, adaptive and self-organising systems

We can recognise the following features most readily in natural systems, but they are equally applicable to purposeful human systems.

Interdependence, cyclical processes and partnership

All members of the system are interconnected in a vast and intricate network of relationships. They derive their essential properties and, in fact, their very existence from their relationships. The success of the whole community depends on the success of its individual members, while the success of each member depends on the success of the community as a whole. An ecosystem's nutrients are continually recycled. Being open systems, all organisms in an ecosystem produce waste, but what is waste for one species is food for another belonging to other natural systems (plants, animals, fungi, bacteria, algae), so that the ecosystem as a whole remains without waste. The cyclical exchanges of energy and resources in an ecosystem are sustained by pervasive cooperation. Competition takes place within a wider order of cooperation. Since the emergence of the first nucleated cells over two billion years ago, Gaia has produced ever more complex arrangements of cooperation and co-evolution.

"Partnership—the tendency to associate, establish links, live inside one another, and cooperate . . . is one of the hallmarks of life."—Fritjof Capra, *The Web of Life*, HarperCollins, London, 1996.

We owe much of the material in this section to Capra's description of systems thinking and how it has contributed to our understanding of the living world.

Flexibility—fluctuation within limits

It is important to know that some limited variation in its key indicators is the sign of a stable system. A system that does not vary is not active. It is switched off, inactive—dead. Our own body temperatures, heart rates and blood sugar levels vary from moment to moment, day to day, year to year. What is true for us is true for all active systems. If, due to something new happening to the system, the variations become too great and exceed the usual limits, then the system changes in some significant way and settles into a new stable state. In its new state there are still slight constant variations but they move between a new set of limits. Think what happens to you as a complex system when you fall in love, lose your job, go through puberty, get a bad attack of malaria or suffer injuries in a car crash. You are still functioning as a system, but your system does not function in the same way as before.

Diversity

A diverse ecosystem will also be resilient, because it contains many species with overlapping ecological functions that can partially replace one another. When a particular species is destroyed by a severe disturbance so that a link in the network is broken, a diverse community will be able to survive and re-organise itself, because other links in the network can at least partially fulfil the function of the destroyed species.

Purposeful human systems as one of Gaia's self-organising sub-systems

Humans are a species of animal that has evolved like any other; the principle of interdependence applies to us with equal force. Our survival and prosperity as a species depend on the continuance of both a living and an inanimate environment capable of supporting human life and enabling it to flourish—in other words, the rest of the Gaian system.

As 'open systems', human societies have the potential to co-create 'virtuous cycles' that largely eliminate waste. We can cooperate with each other and with other species. If we can learn how to make ourselves aware of the limits within which our human systems can operate sustainably, we can avoid de-stabilising the Gaian systems on which we depend.

More advanced systems concepts

Control and order

Engineered systems have predictable outcomes, because all their components can be precisely designed and controlled. Most of our political, administrative, business and NGO leaders assume that purposeful human systems should be as predictable as engineered systems. But it is only as they become **both** increasingly complex **and** increasingly self-organising that purposeful human systems and their component parts also achieve an ordered state, which arises as an emergent property of the system as a whole. As Margaret Wheatley, the American leadership and systems thinker, says: "You can't look at something like self-organisation or complex adaptive systems in science, no matter what unit you're looking [at]—plants, molecules, chemicals—without realising that this is a kind of democratic process. Everybody is involved locally and out of that comes a more global system."[11]

Thus, if we can think of 'democracy' as meaning a system through which members of communities **organise themselves**, rather than a system for controlling them, our democratic systems would be getting closer to being complex, adaptive and self-organising.

Nested systems and recursive organisations

Within every system there are sub-systems, and all the sub-systems have sub-sub-systems, which in turn have sub-sub-sub-systems. In living systems this process takes us from Gaia to single cells and their constituents. In societies, it takes us from governments to individuals. The metaphor of Russian dolls comes to mind, but Russian dolls are the same shape, they have the same pattern. In nature, and in human societies, there are many different kinds of subsystems, many different patterns. Yet although they are nested within each other, all these systems and sub-systems are autonomous and viable. Each can adapt to changes in its environment up to a certain level of complexity.

Human organisations, even the largest of them, have far less inner complexity than their environments. They can only pay attention to selected bits of their environment. The capacity of the leaders of these organisations—governors, directors, managers—is even more limited. They can cope with far less complexity than their organisations as a whole; they must function knowing even less of the detail of the internal and external complexity to which their organisation must relate.

As societies become ever more complex, their leaders have less and less control over the internal and external complexities they face. There is simply too much information for a small group of decision-makers, with limited skills, knowledge and time, to process in order to make confident decisions—no matter how powerful their computers or vast their resources. Thus, if our societies are to be viable parts of the Gaian system, information processing and decision-making power must be devolved as widely as possible. The leaders and the sub-systems can then take actions which aid the viability of the system as a whole.

Organisations that actively seek to devolve their information and decision-making power are known as 'recursive organisations', a term invented by the pioneering British systems thinker, Stafford Beer. And in Chapter 5 we will describe 'network government' and suggest that this is a model Gaian democracies can use to become recursive organisations capable of providing long-term viability.

Matching variety: "variety absorbs variety"
'Variety' is such an important system concept that items beginning 'variety. . .' take up a whole column of references in the index of Beer's *The Heart of the Enterprise*.[12]

One of the best illustrations of how 'variety absorbs variety' is a soccer game. If there are eleven well-trained players on either side, they will more or less match each other, pass for pass, tackle for tackle, shot for shot, save for save. If, say, there are only ten or nine or three players on one side and eleven on the other, the team with the fewer players would be less and less able to 'absorb the variety' (in terms of passes, tackles, shots and saves) generated by the eleven players on the other side.

Now, suppose there are eleven equally talented players on each side, but that the players in one team can only do exactly what the captain tells them to do. Obviously, their opponents would run rings round them, because, within certain fairly loose rules and shared understandings, they would play as a 'complex, adaptive, self-organising system'. By being 'self-organising', the winning team would be able to generate infinitely more variety than the team that could only do what their captain told them.

How could the team that only moved when the captain told them to ever win a match? The captain could try to issue her orders more quickly in a louder voice, using a loudhailer perhaps. Alternatively she might try somehow to reduce the variety generated by the self-organising teams. One way would be to play only opponents who had their ankles tied together. If teams could be found who would agree to being hobbled, it would substantially reduce the variety they could generate. A more realistic solution would be for the captain to stop telling the players what to do and reconfigure their system so that they too became self-organising. It might take some time to learn the new way of playing, but in the end they would start to win matches.

Today we have the all-conquering, self-organising Global Monetocracy Team easily overcoming all opposition. How can the runaway success of the Global Monetocracy be contained and eventually overcome? The answer is that Gaian democracies will somehow have to self-organise and generate sufficient variety to absorb or drastically reduce the variety generated by the Global Monetocracy. Success will not come quickly and easily, but unless we adopt the right tactics in the first place we will never succeed.

Feedback

In everyday speech, being asked to give some 'feedback' means offering our observations or opinions. In non-systems language, 'negative feedback' implies being critical, whereas 'positive feedback' implies being encouraging. In systems terms, 'feedback' is something very different: it means 'a reciprocal (i.e. two-way) flow of influence'. As Peter Senge says, the concept of feedback in a systems context "allows us to see how we are continually both influencing and being influenced by our reality".[13]

Whether the reality concerns the despoliation of the natural world, the impoverishment of rural communities or the narcotics trade, the concept of feedback allows us to go beyond straight-line (or 'linear') cause-and-effect thinking. These and thousands of other problems arise from the dynamic complexity of the system, not from a simple cause and effect process. Thus systems thinking stops us looking for a scapegoat—a person or agency—to blame. Instead, we can see the problems as part of the feedback process being generated by the system as a whole. Consequently, as Senge says: "The feedback perspective suggests that *everyone shares responsibility for problems generated by a system*."[14] [original emphasis]

If 'everyone' is responsible for the problems generated by the system, then 'everyone' is also responsible, somehow, for helping to find ways of tackling them—a profoundly democratic implication.

- **Reinforcing (or positive) feedback**
  Whenever a system is changing faster and faster in one particular direction, reinforcing (or positive) feedback processes are at work. The change could be in terms of increase or decrease, but if the **rate** of change is increasing, then something is **reinforcing** the change process.

  Stock market booms, swarms of locusts and snowballs rolling downhill are examples of reinforcing feedback in action. Whether the spiral is vicious or benign is another matter. The point is that the change will go on indefinitely until the external environment or internal instability brings it to an end. Positive or reinforcing feedbacks are important in the take-off phase of a growing system, but may also be of the vicious sort—this is the 'runaway system' syndrome, which inevitably destabilises both the components of the runaway system and its environment.

- **Balancing (or negative) feedback**
  Balancing (or negative) feedback stabilizes the system and pre-
  vents it running away with itself. All viable systems have balancing feedback mechanisms. They stop the system growing too
  big or exhausting its environment, and aid it to obtain stability.

  Fritjof Capra gives the example of the growth of algae in a
  lake, and the ups and downs of the population of fish that feed
  on it.[15] An unusually warm summer results in increased growth
  of algae in the lake. The fish multiply and consume the algae,
  which is thereby reduced. This is a self-balancing or 'negative'
  feedback loop—'negative' not, of course, in this context imply-
  ing that it's a bad thing. The initial disturbance generates a fluc-
  tuation, which eventually brings the fish/algae system back into
  balance.

  Balancing feedback can only occur when the system is in
  some way goal-orientated. It is a form of self-correction, of steer-
  ing a safe course while maintaining the pursuit of the system's
  intrinsic or innate purpose. At the everyday level, we encounter
  hundreds of balancing feedback mechanisms while doing simple
  things like riding a bicycle. We constantly move our bodies,
  using our weight to stay upright, otherwise a reinforcing feedback would set in, our weight would pull us downwards and we
  would hit the ground. For the human family as a whole to survive, it must use many kinds of balancing feedback mechanisms—in the way food is grown, energy is used and so on.
  Failure to do so can only result in a brutally painful fall.

  Our analysis in Chapter 2 concludes that currently we have
  a runaway system. The only way to avoid the otherwise
  inevitable crash is through the rapid co-creation of Gaian democracies that have the systems knowledge and competencies to put
  in place their own balancing feedback mechanisms.

System delay (lag)

Balancing feedback mechanisms rarely act instantly: they usually take
some time to influence the system. The bigger and more complex the
system is, the longer the delay is likely to be. We have all experienced
system lag when trying to adjust the temperature in the shower. The
water rarely gets hotter or colder immediately; there is always a delay

of a few seconds and, if the water is either scalding or freezing, that can fool us into a cycle of over-adjusting first one way and then the other.

Equally, no matter how effective are the balancing feedback mechanisms set up by Gaian democracies, there will be system delays before they begin to bring our human systems into balance with each other and with Gaia. That is in the nature of complex systems—and the better we, as societies, understand how systems work, the less damaging the delays will be.

Leverage

The concept of leverage comes from engineering but has much wider application. How can we exert the most effective leverage to bring about change? The answer is by applying systems thinking. Failure to use systems thinking when developing solutions to the problems caused by, for example, the current model of economic globalisation—i.e. focusing on the system's emergent properties, rather than their underlying structural causes—can only lead to ineffective, and sometimes gravely damaging, actions. We can only see the structures that have caused the problems if we can find a way of seeing how the whole system is configured. When we can see the whole system we can begin to work out in what way it is giving rise to the problems that are causing so much pain.

Important though it is to alleviate the immediate painful symptoms if at all possible, until we have a grasp of the whole system we will never be able to work out how to tackle their systemic origins. The proposal for Gaian Democracy applies the concept of leverage to finding systemic remedies for the huge number of symptoms that arise from what is loosely called 'globalisation'. By being able to view today's unjust and unsustainable global system—the Global Monetocracy—as a whole, it is possible to strive simultaneously to alleviate the pain of the symptoms **and** to work directly on the systemic changes that are needed to tackle the problems of globalisation.

Soft-systems and hard-systems thinking

Over the past fifty years a variety of approaches have proved to be very fruitful for both understanding how purposeful human systems work and for embarking on the process of reconfiguring them. For convenience, we are bundling these approaches together as 'soft-systems thinking'. The phrase was originally coined by the British systems thinker Peter Checkland, and he has written extensively on the subject.[16] However, we must admit that, by using his terminology as a basis for the reconfiguration of our unjust and unsustainable Global Monetocracy, we are perhaps extending its application some way beyond the point to which Professor Checkland has taken it.

Checkland gives us another useful phrase when he uses 'hard systems' to describe those that are 'engineered' and/or 'mechanistic'. Modern life would be impossible without computers, navigational equipment, oil extraction and refining, satellite and communication systems, transport systems, telecomms, electricity, gas and water supplies—the list is huge. Because of the nature of hard systems themselves—rational, logical and reductionist—hard-systems thinking is extremely effective in producing systems that perform predictably and meet exacting performance criteria.

Unfortunately, the fit between logical, mechanistic, linear hard-systems techniques and the command-and-control values of the business, bureaucratic and political elites, has led to many attempts being made to extend the application of hard-systems thinking from the technical to the human sphere. The results have been increasingly disastrous and embarrassing. As we explain in the next section, it is this failure to understand the need for soft-systems approaches to what systems thinkers call 'wicked' problems that leads to the incompetence of governments in dealing with almost all of the issues on their agenda.

'Wicked' problems and 'tame' problems

Professor Horst Rittel, the German-American systems thinker, pointed out that almost all the major problems that confront our societies can be classified as 'wicked'. That is to say they are problems that arise from non-linear systems' complexities, as opposed to 'tame' problems, which arise from linear system faults. (It should be noted that in systems thinking the terms 'wicked' and 'tame' are used to denote differences in complexity and have no moral or emotional connotations.) What are 'wicked' problems like, and how in practice are they different from 'tame' problems? The main features of 'wicked' problems have been described as follows:

- There is no definitive statement of the problem because it is embedded in an evolving set of interlocking issues and constraints.

- You only begin to understand the problem when you have developed and tested an interim solution.

- There are many people who care about, or have something at stake in, how the problem is resolved, i.e. stakeholders. This makes the problem solving process fundamentally social rather than technical.

- Because there is no objectively 'right answer', what is important is that the stakeholders work out and accept whatever solution looks most promising.

- The constraints on the solution, such as limited resources and political ramifications, change over time. The constraints change—ultimately—because we live in a rapidly changing world. Operationally, they change because many constraints are generated by the stakeholders, who come and go, change their minds, fail to communicate or otherwise change the rules by which the problem must be solved.

- Since there is no objective version of the problem, there is no definitive solution.

- The problem-solving process ends when you run out of time, money, energy or some other resource—not when some perfect solution emerges.[17]

We live in a world full of 'wicked' problems. What should we do as a society about truancy, vandalism, the population explosion, drug dealers, terrorism, racism, over-fishing, global warming, genetic engineering . . . ? The list goes on. These are all 'wicked' problems because they meet the criteria set out above.

'Tame' problems, on the other hand, have definable outcomes and can be objectively solved. Getting rid of a computer virus is a 'tame' problem. Even putting a man on the moon is a 'tame' problem: it is difficult and hugely expensive but if you throw enough time, skills and resources at it you can do it; and you know when you **have** done it.

'Tame' and 'wicked' problems call for totally different approaches. With 'tame' problems there are recognised techniques for identifying and solving the problem. The standard technique is to divide the problem into manageable sub-problems and deal with them in a logical, linear sequence. Dealing with each sub-problem will often call for different kinds of technical expertise. Once all the sub-problems have been solved, the solution to the whole problem is complete. The process is linear. The fatal error is to use linear processes to try to solve 'wicked' problems. Because 'wicked' problems can never be finally 'solved' in the way that 'tame' problems can, soft-systems concepts and methodologies are essential if the stakeholders are to get to grips with them. Because soft-systems thinking is central to Gaian democracies, their approach to wicked problems will make use of these appropriate methodologies and avoid the error of trying to deal with 'wicked' problems as if they were 'tame'.

Soft-systems methodologies

Soft-systems methodologies (or processes) start from the understanding that the 'wicked' problems arising in complex human systems can never be completely and objectively solved. Instead, the people involved in the problem situation are actively involved in a constant cycle of thinking, acting and learning together to understand each other's perspectives, to do what they can to make things better, and then evaluate how successful they have been before starting the process all over again. For this purpose a number of methodologies have been developed by systems scientists and practitioners. The following are some of the most relevant to this Briefing.

- **Defining the system we want to reconfigure**
  The first task is to define the relevant 'system'. Back in the 19th century, the Harvard scientist Josiah Willard Gibbs said that a system is: "Any portion of the material universe [including ourselves and everything we have invented including social systems] which we choose to separate in thought from the rest of the universe for the purpose of considering and discussing the various changes which may occur within it under various conditions."[18] Gibbs' definition is very wide, certainly wide enough to include our democratic systems. But note that he says, "which we choose to separate in

thought from the rest of the universe . . . " and crucially, the concept of a system as an aid to ". . . considering and discussing the various changes which may occur within it under various conditions". The whole business of soft-systems thinking is directed to the question of change within the chosen system.

That is why, when we have to define and agree the boundaries of the system we want to discuss, we are making a subjective decision. There is no objective or scientific set of criteria on which we can take that decision. Instead we have to bring to bear our individual and collective knowledge, concerns, values and visions, and make the choice as best we can. Ultimately, our particular choice is going to depend on what we want the reconfigured system to do, which in turn depends on our shared knowledge, concerns, values and visions. Other groups of people will draw the boundary somewhere else and define the system differently. Moreover, as we understand it—and ourselves—better, we might change our minds and re-define the system yet again. That is in the nature of systems thinking and is what makes it so exciting, creative and, above all, human.

- **Purpose and principles.** In reconfiguring a purposeful human system, the question of its 'purpose' is vital. Dee Hock, the first chief executive of Visa International, and architect of the process leading to its formation, insists that the first two steps are:[19]

1. Develop a statement of purpose. "The first step is to define, with absolute clarity and deep conviction, the purpose of the community. An effective statement of purpose will be a clear, commonly understood statement of that which identifies and binds the community together as worthy of pursuit. When properly done, it can usually be expressed in a single sentence. Participants will say about the purpose, "If we could achieve that, my life would have meaning.""

2. Define a set of principles. "Once the purpose has been clearly stated, the next step is to define, with the same clarity, conviction and common understanding, the principles by which those involved will be guided in pursuit of that purpose. Principles typically have high ethical and moral content, and developing them requires engaging the whole person, not just the intellect. The best will be descriptive, not prescriptive, and each principle will illuminate the others. Taken as a whole, together with the purpose, the principles constitute the body of belief that will bind the community together and against which all decisions and acts will be judged."

Hock warns that, though initially the business of defining the purpose may seem to be difficult and protracted, it pays off handsomely by eliminating many of the difficulties that otherwise arise later in the process. In short, what soft-systems thinking teaches us is that, in reconfiguring 'the system', we—the people involved in the problem—have to work out what we want 'the system' to mean for us, what its purpose should be, and on what principles it should operate.

- **Systems diagrams and rich pictures.** During the last half-century many processes, methods and techniques have been developed. A great deal of expertise has been built up. As Jake Chapman, author of a recent publication for the UK think-tank, Demos, puts it, the main strength of soft-systems methodologies is their "ability to bring to the surface different perceptions of the problem and structure these in a way that all involved find fruitful".[20]

An early task in all soft-systems methodologies is to engage the people in the system in visualising as vividly as possible what they think is going on within the system, and between the system and its environment. No matter how inartistic we think we are, with a bit of coaxing we can all draw some sort of cartoon illustrating our impression of what goes on in the purposeful human system in question. If we draw an essential part of the system as an impassable swamp or a zoo or a black hole, and key personalities as gangsters or the three wise monkeys or babies, some very important information is being conveyed. Much more is revealed about the nature of the system and the people within it by the production of such 'rich pictures' than by simple diagrams with the conventional boxes and arrows—useful though they are at many stages in the process.

Drawing and talking about the very different system pictures and diagrams that we produce are essential if we are to think creatively and purposefully about the complex problems we have to tackle. With system diagrams and pictures we can discuss how one part is related to another, how complete a picture we have of 'the system', how **our** understanding of the system differs from **theirs**, and why.

Discussing our different systems pictures can also profoundly alter our way of thinking about a system that we thought we understood perfectly well before we saw how other people thought about it. Jake Chapman tells how a member of a group of executives included a sketch of an enormous gorilla in his rich picture to represent the boss of a firm with whom he was trying to negotiate a crucial contract. This shocked his colleagues and showed them why they could never seem to reach agreement on this vital issue. One commented, "That one picture saved us many weeks of acrimony and a lot of money."

Gaian democracies as 'soft systems'

Soft-systems methodologies are one of the core components of Gaian Democracy and we will be returning to them in Chapter 5. In our view, by using the vast range of soft-systems methodologies that are already available—and inventing new ones where needed—active citizens can reconfigure our complex human societies to be increasingly adaptive to our relationships with the other parts of the Gaian system. In so doing, our systems of government will become increasingly democratic as millions of active citizens think, act and learn together as they take part in these processes.

To get that far will entail fundamentally reconfiguring the theoretical and practical basis on which today's political and economic systems have been evolved. It is not a question of making even major adjustments to our existing systems—they are impervious to such intentions. As we show in Chapter 3, Western 'democracies' were not designed to fit within the Gaian framework of complex self-organising systems, and have in-built defences against attempts to initiate major changes to their structures and purposes.

"Change in nonlinear systems involves discontinuities, rapid changes as opposed to smooth ones, and persistence; low, for instance, does not necessarily follow high. That is not a comfortable development for people accustomed to promises of order and control, no matter how tenuous. Typically, tiny differences in initial conditions might be magnified, through feedback, into large unforeseen developments."—From: 'Complexity Theory and the Fundamental Challenges to Democracy in the 21st Century'; a paper by Dr. Robert Geyer and Dr. Samir Rihani, presented to the 2000 PSA Conference at the London School of Economics April 2000.

The values that underpin purposeful human systems

We end our outline of the language and concepts of systems thinking with what is possibly the most powerful of all the factors that shape the systems which human beings devise: namely the perspective, the 'worldview' or 'paradigm' of the people who take leading roles. Some paradigms are explicit and conscious belief systems; others are a set of unconscious, unexpressed attitudes internalised into our emotional responses. In both cases they guide our daily actions.

The Canadian philosopher John McMurtry uses the term 'value program' to describe a set of values where people enact its prescriptions and functions as presupposed norms.[21] This is a very useful concept in helping us to understand the mindset and behaviour of the governments of all Western 'democracies' and of the closely associated corporate elites. We use it in Chapter 3, where we suggest the set of values that make up the unifying belief system of contemporary global society. Professor McMurtry does not limit the notion of the value program to government and big business. It extends, he suggests, to the whole of global society. It would include, for example, all the professions, academia (McMurtry has referred to the "wide prison of academic group-think which is almost impossible to penetrate") and almost the whole of 'civil society'.

From the dominant value program, comes the 'purpose' that drives and defines a particular human system; it determines how the system works, and sets limits on the behaviour of everyone within it. These limits are not open to question. It is the purpose—under-pinned by the value program—that explains why political, media and business leaders fail to respond to the major issues facing Gaia and the human family, why they are deaf to warning signs and suggestions for remedial action. Those things are outside their paradigm.

Underlying the conception and implementation of Gaian democracies will be an altogether different set of values and assumptions. Here is an alternative value programme, which Hartmut Bossel proposed as the basis for just and sustainable societies:[22]

- The world is a system of interacting subsystems that have evolved together and depend on each other.

- Society depends on a functioning ecological base and a finite, partly renewable resource-base.

- Future development depends on long-term viability, sustainability and evolutionary potential of the global system and its partner systems.

- The principle of partnership applies to present and future human and non-human systems.

- Diversity of autonomous systems is a prerequisite of sustainable evolution based on the ecological carrying capacity of each region.

- The self-organising potential and diversity of natural evolving systems is seen as the model for the development of sustainable societies.

Summary of Chapter 1

In this chapter we have tried to draw together those basic concepts of systems thinking that are going to be most helpful in enabling us to understand what is happening in the world today, and how purposeful change can be brought about. The more we understand about systems, the better we will be at learning how to create the democracies that will enable our societies to become more just and sustainable. Systems thinking has been successfully applied in many fields; it is now high time that this approach was applied to government and politics.

Chapter 2

Humanity in a Vicious Spiral

Concern about what is happening in the world is usually voiced in terms of environmental issues or social justice—sometimes both, since poverty and degraded environments usually go together. In this chapter we look at some of these same issues in systems terms. This may well prove even more disturbing, but it is an enlightening and necessary starting point from which we can begin to construct an effective strategy for change. We will take environmental issues first and then refer to some social ones. Finally, given that humanity has become such a dominant species, having a significant impact on the Gaian system as a whole, we will look at the broader picture of the current situation and prospects for Gaia.

The meaning you now have in your mind for the word 'environment' will have been enriched by the insights of systems thinking. It no longer stands simply for the natural world out there. It is no longer Nature, as distinct from Man. It is no longer just the environment we know we should be taking better care of, as groups like Friends of the Earth and Greenpeace have been pointing out for at least three decades. For systems thinkers, the word 'environment' is coloured by all we have read in the previous chapter. We are looking now at the Gaian system of innumerable, interdependent living and inanimate systems, and we are seeing the complex web of relationships between them. We know that each system has an internal and an external environment, and that it relates to each of them in complex ways. We know that humans are one of these systems, and that our survival as a species depends on our relationships with all the other systems.

Similarly, we are now seeing social issues not just in terms of justice and human rights. Systems thinking has taught us the importance of looking at these issues in terms of purposeful human systems—social, cultural, economic and political. At the risk of over-generalising, environmental issues could be seen as concerned with the relationships between human societies and the larger systems of which they are part, whereas social issues are concerned with the relationships between human societies and their many sub-systems.

Two crucial factors emerge from our review. The first is the scale and complexity of the whole situation. The more closely we examine the problems, the more frightening they appear to be. And this is not just appearance. One thing you will not get here is some overall explanation that could point towards some overall solution. Precisely the opposite: our first working title for this chapter was "There are no simple answers".

The other crucial factor is that the problems we are facing are not merely technical, economic or legal. They are deeply moral. The extinction of another species, gross inequalities between humans, using up resources so as to deprive future generations: these are issues about which people have strongly held and differing moral views. We are floundering because we don't, at the moment, have adequate ways of addressing these differences constructively. Appeals to people to change their behaviour, whether from campaigning organisations or governments, are bound to fall on deaf ears. Hence the importance of the soft-systems methodologies and the principle of dialogue, in place of monologue, which we will be referring to in Chapter 5. In a nutshell, the global-scale issues now facing the whole of humanity are all 'wicked' problems, calling for governments to tackle them through soft-systems approaches.

However, by looking at what is happening in systems terms we can see some very interesting patterns. The overall pattern we see is, as the title of the chapter says, one of a system in a state of vicious spiral. And that system is one that we have created. That is a very alarming insight. And we should be alarmed, whatever comforting story we may be told by people who want to preserve the existing system of government and economics. Widespread alarm can contribute to the energy leading to change, as we will see in Chapter 6.

Humanity's assault on its own environment

The impact of six billion human beings on the environment is no longer that of bare feet and hands. We still have our ancestors' genes, but our impact is not that of six billion hunter-gatherers. Human identity has been transformed: we have wheels for legs, wings for arms, phones for ears and voices, machines for hands. For naked man we now have what Herbert Girardet calls 'amplified man'.[23] The appendages we use to deliver our assault on our fellow living species and the inanimate resources of the planet are engineered systems. These have become part of our own identity; we can no longer contemplate life without them. We increasingly see the environment on which we depend as an engineered environment. If there are problems ahead we see the solutions in terms of improving the efficiency of engineered systems: using new mining techniques to extract more of the Earth's limited mineral resources, or extracting more from plants by genetic engineering. Linear, hard-systems thinking is not only responsible for the state we are in—it is also seen as the way forward.

Even the most technologically sophisticated of us need to recognise that humanity is one of Gaia's interdependent, adaptive, living systems. We know that in many indigenous civilisations this is fundamental to the way they order their affairs; perhaps some of our own ancestors once thought like this. As city dwellers—now meaning half the world's human population—we have lost direct contact with nature. More significantly, the entire industrialised world is based on, and sees its future in terms of, hard-systems thinking. It is completely unreal to suggest that we could go back to being hunter-gatherers, or indeed to any earlier state of 'civilisation'. Although some of the infrastructure built to service the current industrial system will in due course be dismantled and people may well bring back into use more traditional technologies (made redundant by unsustainable technologies), we cannot undo the technical know-how we have acquired. Hard-systems thinking will certainly continue to be extremely important and useful, but only to solve the 'tame'—not the 'wicked'—problems. What we can, and must, do is to start thinking in soft systems terms about the many 'wicked' problems our 'civilisation' based on hard-systems thinking has landed us with.

Species extinction

Amplified man's assault on our fellow Gaian living systems is nothing less than an ongoing massacre: the indiscriminate and deliberate killing of innocent and defenceless beings; the thought turns the stomach. The description fits; it is not a question of whether the extermination of other species is truly deliberate. That is rather like asking whether a massacre of civilians in some far off country was actually ordered from 10 Downing Street, or the White House or the Kremlin. The point is that these massacres are systemic: they are the inevitable consequence of a system in a state of positive, reinforcing feedback. Individual responsibility is an interesting point, but it is not the important one. What we need to understand, in systems terms, is what makes these massacres inevitable.

Over eleven thousand species of plants and animals (all of which have as much right to live on the planet as we do) are now known to face a high risk of extinction, including 24% of all mammals and 12% of all bird species. The rate of extinction is between 1,000 and 10,000 times faster than it was before human beings began to spread to all corners of the planet.[24] If the current rate of human-induced extinction is allowed to continue, between 10% and 50% of all species will have disappeared over the next 50-100 years.[25] Jeff McNeely, chief scientist to the International Union for Conservation of Nature, has been reported as saying that the next thirty years could be the defining moment for life on Earth. Either we finally recognise the problems and do something about them, or we do not.[26]

Moreover, the interdependence of living species and the balancing feedbacks associated with each species will ensure that each of these extinctions has knock-on effects on the habitats of which they were part; and the destruction of habitats will in turn affect the physical makeup of the soil, the oceans and the atmosphere. The cumulative effects are incalculable.

Destruction or deterioration of ecosystems

In the last 32 years the impact of amplified man has resulted in a 35% deterioration in the Earth's ecosystems.[27] Forest cover has shrunk by 12%, the ocean's biodiversity by a third and freshwater ecosystems by 55%. Data for 350 kinds of mammals, birds, reptiles and fish disclose that the numbers of many species have more than halved. Since 1970, for example, North Atlantic cod stocks have collapsed from an estimated 264,000 tonnes to under 60,000. The environment in which millions of interdependent species exist has thus been drastically changed. Not least that of the human species itself.

Humanity depends on the Earth's biodiversity and on the capacity of ecosystems to survive harvesting, up to certain limits. The sheer stupidity, even in purely economic terms, of human action that reduces biodiversity is illustrated by a recent report showing that the profits from conserving wild places is far higher than the gains made from developing them. Researchers in the US and the UK estimate humanity loses $250bn a result of habitat loss in one year. That loss occurs in the year the destruction happens, and in every subsequent year: they put the cost benefit ratio at more than 100 to 1 in favour of conservation.[28]

According to the US National Academy of Sciences, humans started taking more from the living planet than the planet can replenish in the 1980s.[29] Since then humans have been borrowing against the ecological production of future years. And that is a conservative estimate. It ignores the needs of other species: if 12% of the planet's land and water ecosystems are set aside for wildlife (or, put another way, limiting the dominance of this one species to 88% of the whole!), it was in the 1970s that humans overshot the planet's yearly biological production.[30] That provides a solid scientific justification for E. F. Schumacher's comment in *Small is Beautiful*, published in 1973: ". . . today we are concerned not only with social *malaise* but also, most urgently, with a *malaise* of the ecosystem or biosphere which threatens the very survival of the human race."[31] Future projections suggest that by 2050 humanity's footprint is likely to grow to about 200% of the Earth's biological capacity.[32]

Immediate responsibility for the massive loss of biodiversity lies largely with the industrialisation and commercialisation of agriculture, a process that began 500 years ago with the European conquest of large parts of the Americas, Asia and Africa, and has continued since then at an accelerating pace. For example, in Germany alone, 500 wild plant species are endangered or extinct as a result of agricultural practices. Even more alarming is the loss of biodiversity in the plants we depend on for food. A handful of varieties of most staple crops have now replaced the thousands of varieties that small farmers used to grow. Indian farmers, for example, evolved 20,000 varieties of rice through centuries of innovation and breeding. The loss of such diversity has appalling consequences for rural communities throughout the world, and carries terrifying risks for the safety of food and the security of the food supply for all of us.[33] Meanwhile, thanks to industrial farming methods, 24 billion tons of topsoil—4 tons for every human alive today—washes off the land into the sea every year.[34]

The depletion of inanimate resources

The human assault on our fellow species and ecosystems has been accompanied by—and to a large extent caused by—the plunder of the planet's inanimate resources to fuel industrialisation. While human numbers have increased four-fold in the last century, the resource use of amplified man has increased sixteen-fold.

Of all the Earth's treasures plundered by amplified man, fossil fuels provide the most glaring example of the disastrous limitations of so-called progress based on hard-systems thinking. In practical terms, these are non-renewable resources. And their supply is limited, as we shall soon experience: production of conventional oil is forecast to peak (i.e. to level out and then decline) soon after 2005, to be followed within the next few decades by other types of oil and natural gas.[35] The misuse of fossil fuels for transport and agriculture infringes a basic systems principle, that of the cyclical nature of ecological processes. Quite apart from the immorality of using up resources so as to deprive future generations of their use, and ignoring pollution and global warming, this is suicidal, as the people of North Korea have recently experienced. When imports of oil, on which their mechanised agriculture depended, became unavailable, productivity collapsed. 22 million people starved, three million died. A paper by Tony Boys concludes: "North Korea is an exceptional case only in that, due to political miscalculation and mismanagement of its economy, it has manifested these symptoms before fossil fuel resource shortage becomes a serious concern for the most of the world."[36]

Flying blind

New technologies, while bringing unparalleled health, luxury and comfort for some, can also have a dark side. The biologist Rachel Carson predicted this as long ago as 1963 in *Silent Spring*.[37] Her judgement was based on a systems approach that recognised the balance of nature. In *Our Stolen Future*, Theo Colborn, Dianne

Dumanoski and John Peterson Myers point out that the lethal effects of some man-made chemicals only become apparent after it is too late to recall them. DDT, for example was thought to be safe, and was "spread as liberally as talcum powder across the face of the Earth"[38] before being discovered toxic to wildlife. CFCs were followed by methoxychlor, later found to disrupt hormones. "Like generals, pesticide regulators are always and perhaps inevitably fighting the last war," say the authors.[39] Even after James Lovelock had drawn attention to the ubiquity of CFCs in 1972, it was another two years before environmental chemists Sherwood Rowland and Mario Molina pointed out that CFCs would find their way into the stratosphere and attack ozone.

The approach of the authors of *Our Stolen Future* is also based on systems thinking. "When we conduct experiments on a global scale by releasing billions of pounds of synthetic chemicals, we are tinkering with immensely complex systems that we will never fully comprehend. If there is a lesson in the ozone hole and our experience with hormone-disrupting chemicals, it is this: as we speed towards the future, we are flying blind."[40]

In *Genetic Engineering: Dream or Nightmare?* the biologist Dr Mae-Wan Ho argues that the large-scale release of transgenic organisms is likely to be much worse than nuclear weapons or radioactive nuclear wastes, as genes can replicate indefinitely, spread and recombine. "There may be time enough to stop the dreams turning into nightmares if we act now, before the critical, genetic melt-down is reached."[41] Because genetic structures are biological expressions of the ecosystems which they need in order to survive, genetic engineering, which creates species that could not arise naturally, may have very dangerous impacts on the web of life.[42]

Natural systems cannot be controlled with hard-systems thinking. The very thought should be repellent. The interactions of synthetic chemicals and transgenic organisms with the complex, self-organising systems of the natural world is inherently unpredictable. It is not just a question of a better system of control; what is needed is a better system of government. Since these are 'wicked' problems, this has to be a government system based on soft-systems thinking. Such issues cannot be decided by experts, or politicians relying on experts. They require a process for arriving at purpose and principles, otherwise there is no basis on which to weigh up conflicting considerations. The process must be one where the possibility of an outright, global-wide ban on the creation of further hormone-disrupting chemicals, for example, can at least be on the agenda. That is a challenging demand, but unless we meet it, the only possible future is one where humanity slides further and further away from achieving a stable relationship with the rest of Gaia's systems.

The sickness of societies

Humanity's assault on its environment has been accompanied by an equally devastating assault on itself. Some of the adverse effects are spread fairly evenly. We know, for example, that there is now "no clean, uncontaminated place, nor any human being who hasn't acquired a considerable load of persistent hormone-disrupting chemicals".[43] This applies to every living human on the planet.

Most of the adverse effects are much more selective, with the life circumstances of a large section of the world's population worsening and those of a minority improving. Having said that, it isn't at all clear that even the minority of the world's inhabitants who have become 'wealthier' in the last 35 years are in fact any better off as a result.[44] Pioneering research by the Californian economist Richard Easterlin more than 25 years ago suggested that even though American society was getting richer, people were not becoming any more content with their lot in life.[45] While the motorcar is seen as the main symbol of prosperity today, hyper-mobile societies are anonymous societies; and anonymity breeds crime, fear and paranoia.[46] Most poignant is the effect on children. The surveys carried out by Mayer Hillman, John Adams and John Whitelegg of children's journeys to school in the UK showed that in 1971 80% of 7-8 year-olds were allowed to go to school without adult supervision. By 1990 the figure was 9%; by 2001, 6%.[47]

Worldwide poverty
Through the unrelenting destruction of local cultures, lifestyles, knowledge and communities, we are witnessing the steady erosion of humanity's cultural diversity, flexibility and capacity for self-suf-

ficiency. Due to colonialism and globalisation, local communities have become more and more dependent on systems over which they have little control.[48] In *The Myth of Development* the Peruvian diplomat Oswaldo de Rivero analyses the experience of all so-called developing countries under globalisation. Thirty-seven now have 'non-viable economies'. There is another large group in Latin America, Asia and the Middle East that are incubating symptoms of non-viability. The two groups have in common "an export structure that is technologically dysfunctional with the global economy".[49]

Unemployment, which affects 30% of the world's working-age population, shows no signs of going away. Within the current system, there is no prospect of providing jobs for 700 million unemployed workers. "The greater part of humankind continues to exist with low incomes, in poverty, technologically backward and governed by authoritarian regimes or, at best, in low-powered democracies." For a great many countries, de Rivero concludes, "their only hope will be merely to survive, in some manner, the challenges of the technological revolution and global competition. . . . If their situation should worsen, they could implode into violence, as ungovernable chaotic entities, as has already happened with some countries of Africa, the Balkans, Asia and Latin America."

These very gloomy assessments are echoed by the International Monetary Fund's (IMF) *World Economic Outlook* report for 2000. This noted that, despite the spectacular economic growth of the past century, the quality of life of a fifth of the world's population has actually regressed in relative, and sometimes absolute, terms. This spreading poverty in the midst of economic growth was described by the IMF's deputy research director, Flemming Larsen, as "one of the greatest economic failures of the 20th century".[50]

There has been a huge increase in international inequality. In *100 Ways of Seeing Inequality* the economist Bob Sutcliffe presents compelling evidence of "profound, unacceptable social injustice". In the USA, 10% of the population controls 90% of the nation's wealth.[51] Between 1988 and 2000 the average pay of America's top-ten executives increased from $19.3 million to $154 million, while the majority of Americans lost income.[52] 497 billionaires, at the latest count, share the planet with 1.6 billion people living in extreme poverty.[53] In many countries, black women living in rural areas are the worst affected by extreme poverty. 40% of the world's people suffer from micronutrient deficiencies.[54] Progress in reducing infant and child mortality, and increasing literacy and access to education has slowed during the past twenty years.[55] Globally, 125 million children are deprived of any schooling, another 150 million drop out without learning to read and write. Even in Britain, less than a third of children in the care of local authorities achieve any qualifications when they leave school at sixteen.[56]

Social issues as systemic issues

Many millions of people seethe with righteous anger at the gross injustices they experience in their daily lives. Our brief catalogue has not been anything like comprehensive. We have only just touched on a few of the massive problems confronting us; we have said nothing about war, slavery, population growth, HIV, the explosive growth of cities or world trade. So how does systems thinking help us to relate to this complex mass of frightening problems?

First, just recognising the sheer complexity of it all, the irrationality of the whole scene, is thinking in systems terms. The problems we have mentioned are properties of the current system. It is systems thinking that teaches us to categorise all these problems as 'wicked' problems that cannot usefully be addressed by throwing 'tame' solutions at them. 'Wicked' problems cannot be solved piecemeal by corporately managed technological fixes. We have to look at the systems, because these 'wicked' problems are symptoms of the way that the systems are working.

Take, for example, the population explosion. There are six billion of us already, and there could be ten billion in a few decades. The sheer number of human beings is therefore considered by many to be the biggest single source of pressure on the global environment. Consequently, it is easy to think that this is a 'tame' problem that could be solved by people having fewer children. But, far from being a 'tame' problem, the population explosion is a classic 'wicked' one. It has all the characteristics of 'wicked' problems we set out in Chapter 1. It is one of a large number of 'wicked' problems facing humanity and, once we recognise that, we have taken the first step towards addressing these problems effectively. Continuing to believe that there is a simple answer to any of these problems locks us into a mental cul-de-sac and ensures that we will never escape from it.

Secondly, we can see these social-justice issues in the context of the Gaian complex of interacting, interdependent systems, all in constant flux. The life of every human being, every family, every community and every nation is part of that complex Gaian system. What matters is the health of the whole network of systems.

Thirdly, these social justice issues have practical implications for citizens' ability to participate in the effective working of their societies. As Samir Rihani has pointed out, "The capability of most people in a nation to interact effectively is determined to a large extent by their state of nutrition, health and knowledge. Without that capability they will be powerless to take an active part in the natural evolution of that nation as a complex adaptive system."[57] As Rihani recommends, redistribution of existing financial resources to give priority to basic social programmes would energise the internal dynamics of a nation by boosting the capability of individuals to interact locally.[58]

Prospects for Gaia

The environmental and social problems we have touched on are symptoms of an even wider malaise: amplified man has not yet learned how to co-exist in a balanced relationship with the rest of Gaia's systems. Some of the symptoms relate to humanity's outer environment, some to the co-existence, within the human system, of many sub-systems. In the last part of this chapter we make two further observations about the prospects for the Gaian system as a whole.

Unpredictable effects
The future is essentially unpredictable. At the same time as recognising that Gaia's systems are interdependent, the message from the scientists is that we cannot predict the ultimate consequences of the interaction between interdependent parts of the Gaian system when one part is drastically altered. The balance between tropical rainforests and climate is an example. Recent research suggests that the current process of forest destruction may have consequences far beyond the scientifically predictable effects: the destruction threatens to trigger a

vicious circle of systems collapse within 10-15 years that could lead to total loss of all tropical rainforests within 40-50 years, much sooner than the current rate of loss, taken on its own, would suggest.[59]

Similarly, some scientists consider that global warming may lead to the collapse of the Western Antarctic Ice Sheet, resulting in a global sea-level rise of six metres (!!).[60] There is also a danger of large areas of permafrost melting, which would release massive amounts of methane, a very powerful greenhouse gas.[61] Global warming could become a positive feedback, unstoppable by any form of human intervention.

Sometimes, the best the scientists can do is to warn us to expect disasters. We know that industrialisation has resulted in an increase in the concentration of 'greenhouse gases' in the Earth's atmosphere. The consequences are already being widely experienced: there was, for example, a sharp rise in the late 1990s in the number of weather-induced disasters. According to the annual *World Disasters Report* of the International Federation of Red Cross and Red Crescent Societies, floods, storms, landslides and droughts, which numbered about 200 a year before 1996, rose steadily to 392 in 2000. Latest reports confirm that global warming is accelerating.[62]

A Gaian system-shift

Scientists can often see certain patterns in the way systems behave. One of these is that when a system ceases to maintain a balanced relationship with its environment, it tends to shift its form quite suddenly. For some closely dependent systems the consequences can be severe, and even fatal. Applied to the Gaia system as a whole, this suggests we can expect some rude shocks.

Gaia herself has illustrated this pattern many times. Small shifts in the angle of the Earth's axis in its 100.000 year orbit of the Sun coincide with the onset and ends of ice-ages. There have been ten ice ages over the past million years. An ice age lasts for about 100,000 years, and is followed by 10-15,000 year 'inter-glacial period'. We are in an inter-glacial period now, and have been for about 12,000 years.

If the Earth followed its `normal' pattern, a new 100,000 year ice-age would not be due to start for another 2000 years or so. But some climate scientists calculate that the existing warming trends might bring one on prematurely. Then, the shift from inter-glacial to ice age will happen with remarkable speed—in a matter of a few decades.

Over a few hundreds or thousands of years after a Gaian shift, thousands of species die off or migrate to new habitats. Gradually everything settles down to this new norm. Then, if the changes in the chemical composition of the atmosphere are reversed, air and sea temperatures rise by a few degrees, the biological systems respond to those variations, and the balance swings the other way. The ice-sheets melt, the seas flood in to cover the low-lying coastal lands and everything settles down again for tens of thousands of years—until the change swings back again. And then again. And so it goes on.

The first time that organised human societies endured a major shift in the Gaian system was between 12,000 and 15,000 years ago. That was when the vast mile-deep ice-sheets that had covered large parts of what are now Canada, the USA, Europe and Russia for nearly 100,000 years started to melt. We have some idea of the effects of the last Gaia system-shift from the stories of the Flood that are embedded in the folk-tales of the societies that have survived from that era.

Over the past 10,000 years or so most human societies have moved from simple hunting and gathering, through agriculture to industrialisation. During that time the Gaian systems we depend on have been in a stable, but slightly fluctuating, balance with each other. The average yearly temperature, and the chemistry of the sea and the air have varied only slightly from year to year. Today, as the by-products of our industrialised societies are rapidly changing the chemical composition of the air, the variations in the temperature of the air and the sea are becoming much greater. Such temperature changes have massive effects on Gaia's biological systems. In their turn, those changes amplify the changes in the carbon dioxide and methane content of the air. As these dynamic feedback processes interact with one another, the Gaian systems are increasingly de-stabilised. Research carried out at Stanford University in California confirms, as we would expect, that the effects of interfering with Gaia's interactive systems are complex. As Harold Mooney, the Paul S. Achilles Professor of Environmental Science at the university cautioned: "There is still a lot to learn about the factors that regulate global climate change." [63]

The air bubbles trapped in the Arctic ice tell us that over the past

200,000 years the natural rates of world wide temperature change are typically about one degree Centigrade every thousand years or so. Today the rate of change in global temperatures is far faster. Mathematical models of the climate suggest that if carbon dioxide levels double sometime in the middle of this century, the world will warm between one and five degrees Centigrade. The mild end of that range entails warming at the rate of one degree per hundred years—**ten times faster** than the average natural rate. Should the higher end of the range occur, we could see rates of climatic change fifty times faster than natural average conditions.[64]

The changes in the temperature and the chemistry of the sea and the air are thus signalling that a major shift in the Gaian system-balance may be about to happen. This could accelerate the start of another ice age, or it could precipitate a return to the much warmer and wetter global climate that was last seen millions of years ago. Whichever way it goes, all forms of life on Earth will have to respond to massive climatic changes. If, as the models suggest, these changes are likely to happen ten to fifty times faster than they did before human beings started building industrial societies, the rate of extinction of species of all kinds is likely to be many times higher than the already horrendous rate of today.

The impact on human societies is bound to be immense and could well be fatal in many areas. We must hope that the full impact of the coming system-shift will take several hundred years to get underway. However, it could well kick in within the next fifty years or even sooner. If past performance is anything to go by, once a Gaian system-shift gets fully into its stride it will move into its new and very different stable state in a matter of a few human generations: 50-100 years at most.

James Lovelock's key insight was that living things have been the main influence on the Earth's climate over the past four billion years. One particular species is now taking the lead in this. As the authors of *Our Stolen Future* have stated: "The unprecedented and awesome power of science and technology, combined with the sheer number of people living on the planet, have transformed the scale of our impact from local and regional to global. With that transformation, we have been altering the fundamental systems that support life. These alterations amount to a great global experiment—with humanity and all life on Earth as unwitting subjects." [65]

In conducting this 'experiment' we are breaching a number of the principles we learned from studying living systems: we are ignoring the fact that all systems are interdependent; and we are using competition instead of partnership and co-operation. Every loss of biodiversity or cultural diversity reduces the flexibility that is the greatest strength of any system, especially in times—like the present—when its environment can be expected to inflict sudden changes.

The Scientists' Warning

In 1997, 1,670 scientists including 110 of the 138 living winners of Nobel prizes in the sciences, issued this warning: *"We are fast approaching many of the Earth's limits. Current economic practices which damage the environment cannot continue. Our massive tampering could trigger unpredictable collapse of critical biological systems, which are only partly understood. A great change in our stewardship of the Earth and the life on it is required if vast human misery is to be avoided and our global home on this planet is not to be irretrievably mutilated."*—Union of Concerned Scientists. See *www.ucsusa.org/ucs/about/page.cfm?pageID=1007*

Conclusion

Why are we failing to observe basic systems principles even though we are the one species that has developed a brain capable of understanding what we are doing? It must surely be because we have a system of ordering our affairs that not only perpetuates and aggravates these catastrophic trends, but that also conceals, distorts and misrepresents what is going on. That is why we must now try to pin down exactly what this system is and what makes it work in the way it does—and then try to work out how to reconfigure it.

Chapter 3
The Global Monetocracy

It is clear from Chapter 2 that there is indeed a lot wrong with the world. There is every justification for deep concern. In this chapter we will discover that the appalling symptoms we have seen, diverse though they are, are not separate: **they all stem from the purposes, principles and ideologies of a purposeful human system**.

In this chapter we will see that the responsible system is a vast and complex 'Global Monetocracy' that affects the life of every human being and the rest of nature within the Gaian system. It is this Global Monetocracy that is inflicting the increasingly severe and disabling injuries to which we have drawn attention.

Because the Global Monetocracy is so complex, it is important to sketch its main components and think through how they interact. Once we have a rough outline of the whole system and its interactions, we have some idea of what it will take to dismantle and replace it with something better. However formidable that task may be, realising what has to be done takes us halfway towards relieving our sense of impotence. We are seeing the world in a different way.

If we are correct in saying that the Global Monetocracy as a whole is responsible for what is happening, it follows that **it is the Global Monetocracy as a whole that must be reconfigured**. The next step will be to begin to work out how, and by whom, the system can be reconfigured. That is the task we tackle in Chapter 5.

The Global Monetocracy

Today's government and economic systems have co-evolved over the last four hundred years. They are now so tightly enmeshed as to form a single integrated system, the components of which are shown in **Figure 1**. Interlocked and interdependent, each contributes in its own way to a system that is driving the destabilising and destructive trends we have identified.

FIGURE 1. The main components of the Global economic/political Monetocracy

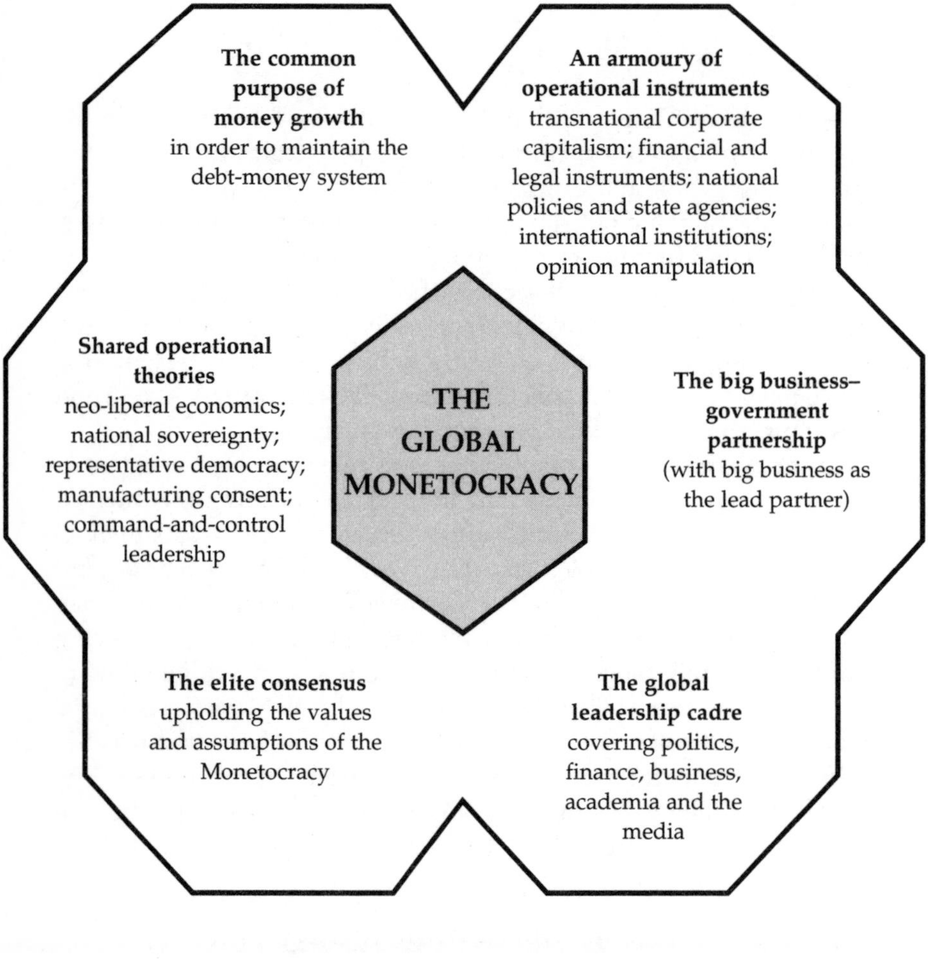

The common
purpose of
money growth
in order to maintain the
debt-money system

An armoury of
operational instruments
transnational corporate
capitalism; financial and
legal instruments; national
policies and state agencies;
international institutions;
opinion manipulation

Shared operational
theories
neo-liberal economics;
national sovereignty;
representative democracy;
manufacturing consent;
command-and-control
leadership

**THE
GLOBAL
MONETOCRACY**

The big business–
government
partnership
(with big business as
the lead partner)

The elite consensus
upholding the values
and assumptions of the
Monetocracy

The global
leadership cadre
covering politics,
finance, business,
academia and the
media

Main components of the Global Monetocracy

Component 1: The purpose of the Global Monetocracy

The common purpose of money growth in order to maintain the debt-money system

The defining component of any purposeful human system is its purpose. The purpose of the economic system promoted by all Western governments is never debated. It is nowhere even acknowledged. You will not find it written over the door of any presidential office, state legislature or party political headquarters. Nevertheless, in our judgement, the true purpose of the Global Monetocracy, is that of **money growth in order to maintain the current debt-based money system**.

What is our evidence for this assertion? The debt-money system itself has been described in earlier Schumacher Briefings by James Robertson and Richard Douthwaite. They show that almost all the money we use (i.e. all except the notes and coins, which today are about 3% of the total) came into existence as a result of a bank agreeing to make a loan to a customer, at interest. This is why it is called 'debt-money'.[66]

This system has several extremely important consequences. First, it gives the banks a free lunch. They are, in effect, able to print money and lend it out at interest. Bank profits from this source alone in the USA, UK, Eurozone and Japan are about $140 billion per year.[67] It is quite outrageous that the banks should have this power. Counted among public figures that have been bold enough to object are three US presidents: Thomas Jefferson, Abraham Lincoln and Franklin Roosevelt. Its many critics amongst economists have even included Milton Friedman, a favourite of Margaret Thatcher and the American Right.[68] That the governments of Western 'democracies' permit the banks to continue to enjoy this massive subsidy, and for this extraordinary privilege to be off the agenda of public debate, is a tribute to the power of the 'elite consensus' discussed later in this chapter.

Secondly, the effect of this method of creating money is that the economy has to grow in order to avoid collapsing. In industrial countries, between 18% (Sweden) and 26% (Japan) of each year's total output is ploughed back into investment projects. If in any year this figure falters, the economy risks entering a downward spiral. The fact that the necessary growth can be achieved only by increasing the total level of debt makes the economy heavily dependent on confidence. People borrow when they are optimistic about being able to repay with interest. Businesses borrow when they want to expand. Confidence in the future is self-fulfilling. So is the lack of it. The economy therefore constantly moves between boom and bust; it is systemically unstable.

Consider what happens if growth slows or stops. First of all unemployment appears. Firms that invested in the past in the expectation of increasing sales find themselves with surplus capacity, and consequently cancel further investment projects. This puts the people who would have designed, constructed and equipped them out of work. So for the government, no growth or slow growth means rising unemployment and, as a result, higher social welfare bills. Also, because wages, turnover and business profits fall away, it means lower tax receipts. The public finances go into the red, and the government has to choose between increasing tax rates or borrowing, thus increasing the National Debt. The policies of the party in office lose all credibility, making it unlikely to be returned at the next election.

The consequences for the business sector are even more serious. Since interest has to be paid on most of the money invested in the failed expansion projects, corporate profits tumble. The developing recession cuts the value of investment properties, land, antiques, fine art. Even the housing market collapses because of the rising unemployment, leaving millions with negative equity.

The worst danger of all is that the economy falls to the sort of level it reached in the 1930s and that high levels of unemployment persist for several years. This would throw the viability of the entire capitalist system into question—a frightening thought for those who owe their power to it. Not surprisingly, the possibility of a down-ward spiral is a prospect that terrifies governments. That is why—whatever their political colour—governments try to work closely with the business sector. In this way they can ensure that, regardless of any social or environmental damage, the economy continues to grow. The debt-money system thus forces governments to put the imperative for short-term growth above long-term considerations of justice and sustainability.

Governments are quite open about the need for economic growth. But what they hardly ever admit is that this need is imposed by the debt-money system, let alone that this method of creating money is quite unnecessary and certainly contrary to the interests of the taxpayer and the public generally.[69] And they will of course always contend that growth will benefit people directly, even though the opposite has been shown to be the case in many countries over the last few decades.[70]

Nor is it true, as our current leaders invariably assert, that economic growth is necessary for human development in poorer countries. In *Complex Systems Theory and Development Practice*, Samir Rihani has provided compelling evidence that, for nations where the need for human development is most desperate, economic growth is largely irrelevant and possibly wasteful.[71]

Furthermore, it is the banks, rather than governments, who shape the way the economy develops, because a high volume of bank lending—which the banks control—is essential if the present money system is to function. They determine who can borrow and for what purpose, according to criteria which favour those with a strong cash flow or substantial collateral. Justice and sustainability are irrelevant. The system thus favours rich people and multinational companies against smaller firms and poorer individuals. It gives an automatic advantage to the wealthy and thus tends towards ever-greater inequality. It also totally ignores Gaia.

In systems-thinking terms, the growth imperative imposed by the debt-money system is a positive feedback mechanism—a vicious spiral. It is also a classic case of leverage: the leverage that the debt-money system exerts on national economies and on the global economy as a whole leads directly to the effects we outlined in Chapter 2.

Debt-money is also the ideal instrument for imposing a stranglehold of debt on the world's poorest countries.[72] It forces them to increase their exports, thus drawing down commodity prices for the benefit of wealthier countries. It is the basis of the global financial system in which, year after year, money flows not from rich countries to poor countries but in the opposite direction.[73] It is the source of the system's instability, the main impact of which always falls on the poorer countries and on the poor in those countries.

Linked to the debt-money system is the use of the currencies of some of the wealthiest countries (US dollars, UK sterling, Euros, Japanese yen and Swiss francs) as 'reserve currencies', so-called because they are held by central banks as reserves. These are national currencies being used as though they were global currencies. Around 70% of all foreign currency reserves held by central banks are US dollars. In effect, the system enables a wealthy country to import goods from, or acquire assets in, a poorer country, without 'paying' for them. For example, Japan can import goods from an African country and pay for the goods in yen. These cost Japan nothing to print, or more probably, to create with an electronic entry. If those yen remain in the central bank of the exporting country, or if they are kept in a bank in Japan in an account controlled by the African country or a member of its ruling elite, or if they are used to buy investments in Japan, it follows that Japan never has to export anything in return. The effective cost to the Japanese economy is nil.

Between 1992 and 2000, the number of US dollars held as reserves by central banks around the world grew by $800 billion, an average of $100 billion a year. This constituted an $800 billion interest free loan by the rest of the world to the USA. In effect the USA has been able to buy $800 billion worth of goods and foreign assets without paying for them. It has been described as a tribute, a crippling tax that the rest of the world pays to the USA. For the USA, it is another case of a free lunch.[74]

Even that isn't all, because almost all those dollars were created by US banks as debt. Richard Douthwaite has calculated that the total return to the USA from creating the money is of the order of $425 billion **per annum**. This has enabled the USA to run a trade deficit in the order of $1.2 billion per day. Compare that with the figure of $343 billion for the US military budget for 2002.[75] It is a country that has been able to build its military strength at the expense of the rest of the world—not so much a free lunch as a free army, navy and airforce.

Yet, while the world was paying the USA a $425 billion per annum tribute, US aid to 'developing' countries was running at around $10 billion per annum. The USA, by far the wealthiest country in the world, is the donor country that gives away by far the lowest proportion of its national product[76]—over the last half century the proportion has declined from 0.3% to 0.1%.[77] "What a peculiar world," comments Joseph Stiglitz, former Chief Economist of the World Bank and Chair of President Clinton's Advisory Committee on the Economy, "in which the poor countries are in effect subsidising the richest country, which happens at the same time to be amongst the stingiest in giving assistance in the world."[78]

The purpose of the Global Monetocracy explains why, for example:

- Our governments have persistently ignored all the evidence of the adverse effects of economic growth, including the repeated warnings of scientists over the last forty years.

- Our governments continue to claim that economic growth is the only viable strategy for tackling the world's horrific agenda of problems that have—in large part—been caused by the self-same economic growth.

Note that what we have been looking at here is the **purpose** of the Global Monetocracy **as a system**. What we have named as the Global Monetocracy is the aggregate of the components shown in Figure 1 (page 68). The purpose of that aggregate system is not the same thing as the conscious purpose of any player in the system. This is not a conspiracy theory: it is a statement about a system.

The purpose of a system does however have a controlling influence on the way the whole system works, and hence on the behaviour of all players in it. That of course is why we have called the system a 'Global Monetocracy'.

FIGURE 2. Component 2: Shared operational theories

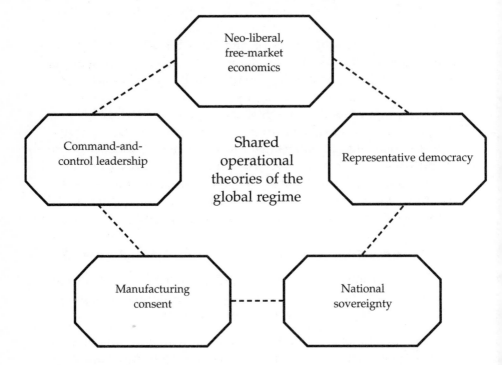

Component 2: Shared operational theories
Underlying the purpose of the Global Monetocracy, and providing the basis for its claim to intellectual respectability, legitimacy and competence, are a number of key operational theories.

It is a striking fact that all of these theories are currently in crisis. Neo-liberal economics is fatally flawed both by its own standards and by the yardsticks of justice and sustainability; nation-states are dominated by multinational corporations and cannot grapple with the regional and global issues confronting the human family; voters are disenchanted with the kind of politics produced by traditional representative democracy; command-and-control leadership methods are increasingly less effective in complex modern societies; and the manufacture of consent no longer provides a reliable basis for social control. The inadequacies of each of these theories will now be spelt out in a little more detail.

- **Theory 1: Neo-liberal economics.** Since the late 1970s, neo-liberal economic ideology has shaped the policies of almost all Western 'democracies'. Its principles include the primacy of private property, economic growth, the need for free trade to stimulate growth, competition, the unrestricted 'free-market', privatisation and the absence of government regulation. The theory is a highly selective interpretation of the classical, mainstream tradition of economics.

  The success of what John Maynard Keynes called "this misleading and disastrous" economic ideology is not an accident.[79] It is the result of a concerted, well financed, utterly determined and increasingly globalised campaign led originally by the Austrian economist Frederick von Hayek, his colleague, Milton Friedman, and other members of the so-called 'Chicago School'. It is a theory of economics deliberately developed to serve the interests of the owners of capital. It serves as a rationale to justify the money growth economy.

  As early as 1947, Hayek founded The Mount Pelerin Society, which brought American and European conservatives together in a village near Lausanne, Switzerland. As Susan George has revealed, Americans who attended that first Mount Pelerin Society meeting had their travel and accommodation expenses paid for by the William Volker Fund.[80] Volker money also bailed-out shaky free-market academic magazines, financed the books published by the Chicago School, paid the bills for the influential Foundation for Economic Education and funded meetings of free-market thinkers at US universities.

  The Mount Pelerin Society inspired friendships, networks and joint projects, and has remained an international club for free-market thinkers ever since. Membership of the society is by invitation and—significantly—the members' names are not disclosed, though it is known that members have included the Thatcherite Czech ex-Prime Minister, Vaclav Klaus, the former French finance minister, Alain Madelin, Boris Yeltsin's chief advisers and, of course, Margaret Thatcher.

  The opinion-moulding strategy that was launched in the late 1940s is being pursued with undiminished vigour to this day. Hundreds of millions of dollars are spent every year to enable

The Mount Pelerin Society and the scores of other free-market institutions that follow its lead to maintain their dominance of the field.[81]

By the mid-1980s, adherence to free-market neo-liberal economic ideology had become the benchmark for the credibility of finance ministers, treasury mandarins, professional economists and 'expert' economic advisers throughout the industrialised world. This was despite the fact that since the middle of the 19th century the deficiencies of neo-classical economics have been extensively documented. As many eminent economists have shown, the proposition that a market economy necessarily maximises commercial efficiency and social welfare is not true, even in theory.[82] Even international financier George Soros agrees that fundamentalist market ideology—blind faith in free, unfettered markets—is supported by neither modern theory nor historical experience.

Neo-liberalism is a theory of economics that is totally divorced from living systems. Professor John McMurtry has described it as "an economic paradigm that has no life co-ordinates." For McMurtry, 'life values' include ecology and 'non-profit' work, things that are not monetized and hence not valued by markets.[83] Neo-liberal economics is thus blind to Gaia and to the damage its application does to the moral, social and ecological dimensions of our human and natural worlds. The evidence of the destruction inevitably caused by the application of neo-liberal economic theory, and of the repeated failure to achieve even declared objectives, is overwhelming, yet this paradigm nevertheless sets the parameters of acceptable political and democratic thought. It resembles a religious theology that provides its priesthood with an unchallengeable but entirely metaphysical authority; neo-liberal economists are the priests promoting that religion and not, as they claim, scientists seeking to understand the nature of the world they purport to explain and predict.

- **Theory 2: Representative democracy.** At the opening of the 21st century, 120 out of the 192 countries of the world, containing some 60% of the world's population, were ruled by representative democracies. This system is generally portrayed as the enlightened alternative to totalitarian dictatorships, theocracies and military governments. It is held up as being the only way people in modern societies can govern themselves, the only practicable form democracy can take in the modern world.

Traditional representative democracies are, however, perfectly suited to the Global Monetocracy, because they are designed to minimise public involvement in government, and to enable the dominant elite to remain continuously in control. The system provides the constitutional framework that has enabled the elite to force neo-liberal economics on a world that naturally resists it. As John Gray, Professor of European Thought at the London School of Economics, has pointed out: "Free markets are creatures of state power, and persist only so long as the state is able to prevent human needs for security and the control of economic risk from finding political expression. Encumbered markets are the norm in every society, whereas free markets are the product of artifice, design and political coercion. Laissez-faire must be centrally planned; regulated markets just happen. The free market is not, as Right-thinkers have claimed, a gift of social evolution. It is an end product of social engineering and unyielding political will. It was feasible in 19th century England only so long as functioning democratic institutions were lacking."[84]

The key role of the ordinary citizen in representative democracies is to vote at elections. But while the choice at elections is increasingly meaningless, citizens are still regarded as having had their say as voters. The vast majority of ordinary citizens are still excluded from active participation in governmental decision-making at all levels. Contact with ordinary people is limited to focus groups, opinion polls and consultation. There is no room for citizen initiative. The result, inevitably, is a largely passive and disillusioned citizenry. This has led to mass abstention from the system, with over 50% of voters in the USA staying away from the polls. Membership of political parties in Europe has plummeted. The picture is similar throughout Latin America and Eastern Europe.[85]

Amongst politicians, those with the most money and the best connections are especially favoured. Moreover the system provides easy access for big business to government through electoral funding, lobbying and policy-making processes that are specially designed to be business-friendly.

Representative democracy thrives on carefully chore-ographed displays of adversarialism and inter-party competition. It legitimises secrecy and censorship. It facilitates the manipulation of public opinion. Public debate is effectively infantilised.

The critical link between politicians and the people is now the focus group, originally devised for companies to discover how to package products so that they overcome potential customers' resistance to them. Several decades ago political consultants spotted that elections are won and lost by the largely self-interested preferences of the small minority of so-called 'swing voters'. Swing-voters have no party loyalties and it is their votes that 'swing' elections by a few percentage points one way or the other. As Robin Cook, Leader of the House of Commons and a member of the New Labour elite, has said: "The reason why, at election time, we chase those 0.25% of the electors who are the crucial swing voters in the crucial target seats, is that ultimately they are the only ones whose votes matter."[86] From their studies of voting patterns, electoral strategists have persuaded political leaders that they have to listen to, and rapidly satisfy, the desires and prejudices of swing voters. The consequence is that policy is made on the basis of last month's focus group results, and all parties strive to get closest to the swing voters at whatever cost to their principles, the loyalty of their 'traditional' supporters or the interests of the community as a whole.

Once the focus group strategists have identified the messages that are most likely to appeal to swing voters, huge sums are spent on advertising targeted at them. Candidates in the 2002 congressional and gubernatorial races in the USA spent close to $1 billion for television commercials alone. In the UK, having won power by using these methods, New Labour leader, Tony Blair, was able to say: "I have taken from my party everything they thought they believed in. What keeps it together is success and power." [87]

Representative democracy has many other flaws. Elections, which allegedly protect the people from abuse of power, are frequently manipulated by those in high office in order to prolong their power. And, as we saw in the UK following the Falklands War, and in the 2002 mid-term elections in the USA, wars and threats of war favour the party in office. It pays today's political leaders to pretend there is a crisis, or a threat the nation's prosperity or pride. Presidents Bush and Mugabe have proved that it pays to manufacture such a crisis. The link here with the 'manufacture of consent' (see below) is obvious.

Regular elections also invariably ensure that elected politicians concentrate on producing a stream of uncoordinated policy initiatives to placate the swing voters, ignore the long-term consequences of their policies and generate ever-greater complexity and confusion.

As we shall see in Chapter 5, the proposition that representative democracy is the only practicable form of democracy in today's world is nonsense. It is one of the many myths promoted by the Global Monetocracy for its own protection.

- **Theory 3: National sovereignty.** Nation-states have co-evolved with representative democracies as the official vehicles and processes whereby our societies are dominated by a wealthy elite. The dominance of today's political, corporate, financial and media elites is in a direct line from the role played by monarchs, courtiers, landowners, bankers and merchants in the 17th, 18th and 19th centuries. The purpose of the nation-state was to enable the elites to sustain their power and privileges through constant territorial and economic expansion.[88]

The principle of national sovereignty is inherently conflictual and competitive. It cuts across natural diversities of culture and geography. It fosters nationalism, illusions of moral superiority and dreams of empire. At the same time, under the cloak of national sovereignty, the nation-state provides the executive and legislative support required for the monetisation and corporate ownership of the entire human and natural worlds.[89]

As with all the components of the Global Monetocracy, it is the way in which they operate together that matters. As John

Gray has pointed out, the global free market works to set sovereign states against one another in a struggle for dwindling natural resources.[90] The effect is to impel states to become rivals for the control of resources that no democratic institution has the responsibility for conserving. In this struggle the already wealthier states inevitably win. It is a recipe for ever-greater economic and political instability. Rich countries can afford to mitigate, at least temporarily, the penalties that global free markets impose on their citizens. In poorer countries the global free market produces fundamentalist plutocracies and works as a catalyst for the disintegration of traditional societies.

From a systems perspective, one of the most serious defects of the principle of national sovereignty and the nation-state system is that it has blocked the development of democracy for the human family as a whole. Once the elites had chosen to conceive of the human family as a collection of states, responsibility for organising the interaction between human societies became the preserve of state governments. According to Philip Allott, Professor of International Public Law at Cambridge University: "The result was that we came to have an international system which was, and is, post-feudal society set in amber— undemocratised, unsocialised—capable only of generating so-called *international relations*, in which so-called *states* act in the name of so-called *national interests*, through the exercise of so-called *power*, carrying out so-called *foreign policy* conducted by means of so-called *diplomacy*, punctuated by medieval entertainments called *wars* or, in the miserable modern euphemism, *armed conflict*. This is the essence of the social process of the international non-society."[91]

In other words, on the global stage there is no democracy at all. Nothing could be better suited to the advancement of the purpose of the Global Monetocracy, led by largely uncontrolled transnational corporations operating in a largely unregulated global marketplace. The 1992 Earth Summit in Rio de Janeiro highlighted the weakness of state governments faced with strong lobbying by transnational corporations. Corporations and their lobby groups easily ensured that any consideration of binding regulation of transnational companies was excluded from the programme endorsed by the so-called, but misnamed, 'world leaders'.[92]

In the decade since Rio the absence of any global democracy has allowed corporations the political space to manoeuvre them-selves into decision-making positions on vital global issues. The outcome is the current programme for the further commodifica-tion and privatisation of nature launched at the 2002 World Summit on Sustainable Development at Johannesburg.[93]

- **Theory 4: Manufacturing consent.** During World War One, the British government was desperate for the USA to declare war on Germany. Stories of atrocities by the Germans, or 'Huns' as they were called, were fabricated by the British propaganda ministry. Belgian babies with their arms torn off, speared on bayonets, and Belgian and French women raped in their thousands featured prominently in American newspapers. This was part of the British High Command's highly successful effort "to control the thought of the world".[94]

Britain's aim was to control the thought of the more intelli-gent members of the community in the US. If they could be per-suaded to disseminate British propaganda, they might succeed in converting the pacifist USA to wartime hysteria. The USA entered the war against Germany in 1917. The strategy had worked brilliantly. And it taught every other nation a lesson. The lesson was that when state propaganda is supported by the edu-cated classes, and when no deviation is permitted, it can have a big effect on public opinion.

The success of Britain's propaganda campaign in WW1 has inspired all the state propagandists down to the present day: from Hitler's Goebbels to Tony Blair's Alistair Campbell, although, of course, with the spread of radio, TV and the cinema, the techniques have been constantly refined.

By the early 1920s, propaganda had been re-branded as 'public relations' and the lessons learnt from Britain's success in dragging the USA into the first World War gave rise to some-thing much more powerful than mere imitation: it spawned a theory. In 1922, the young Walter Lippman, later to be the most revered of American political journalists, saw himself as a theorist of modern democracy. In his immensely influential book, *Public Opinion*, he argued that public relations amounted to a "revolution in the art of democracy", and could be used to "manufacture consent".[95] In other words, the new techniques of public relations could be used to persuade the voters to agree to policies that they didn't want. The theory of manufacturing consent rested on Lippman's proposition that "in a properly-functioning democracy" there are three distinct classes of citizens.

First of all, there is the specialised class: the citizens who take some active role in running general affairs—what today we would call the ruling elites, or perhaps 'the Establishment'. The second class are the decision-makers: the people who analyse, execute, make decisions and run things in the political, economic, and ideological systems; in other words, the public officials, bureaucrats and apparatchiks. Then there is what Lippman called "the bewildered herd", the vast majority of citizens who have been excluded from playing any meaningful role in the government of their society. By 'manufacturing consent' through public relations (i.e. propaganda) techniques, the specialists and decision-makers could tame the bewildered herd into acquiescence. Today, state and corporate public relations is a huge industry. Billions of dollars a year are spent in trying to control the public mind. And, as Noam Chomsky says, "Propaganda is to democracy what the bludgeon is to a totalitarian state." [96]

Fortunately, however, we—the bewildered herd—are never properly tamed. When large numbers of us can get together—in political campaigns, trade unions, colleges or churches—we sometimes refuse to allow our consent to be manufactured; and then our leaders tell us that we are creating 'a crisis of democracy'.[97] In fact, by forcefully—but non-violently—expressing our collective views we are doing what citizens in democracies are supposed to do. But, in the emasculated version of democracy that has co-evolved with the Global Monetocracy over the past four hundred years, by expressing our fundamental disagreement with the actions of the Government, we are being 'anti-democratic'. The sooner we are driven or bamboozled back to the apathy, obedience and passivity of the bewildered herd, the better.

Identical methods of manufacturing consent are now used by political parties, government bodies and private corporations.[98] In the case of business, the purpose is to create the consumer demand that the growth economy craves. In the case of the political parties and public bodies, it is to secure the public's acceptance of their own exclusion. The US media analyst, Ben Bagdikian, sums it all up by saying that the institutional bias of the mass media "does not merely protect the corporate system. It robs the public of a chance to understand the real world".[99]

The manufacture of consent is in fundamental opposition to the concept of a learning society. Increasingly though, the crisis in the theory of manufacturing consent is deepening. The old maxim that "you can't fool all of the people all of the time" is coming home to roost. The consequence is that the drive to "get across the government's message" and keep the bewildered herd under control, has become increasingly desperate, obvious and counter-productive.[100]

- **Theory 5: Command-and-control leadership.** The message that hundreds of millions of voters, otherwise known as the bewildered herd, are given by their political leaders is the same message that generations of employees have been given by their bosses. The message is: "We don't need you to think! We need you to do what we tell you. If there's any thinking to be done around here, we'll do it." That, in essence, is how command-and-control leadership operates. As consultants Dean Anderson and Linda Ackerman Anderson have written: "Command-and-control is by far the most common leadership style. Most of today's leaders were mentored themselves by command-and-control managers, and the culture of most organizations is still based on command-and-control norms. It is hard to escape this leadership style's historic influence and dominance."[101]

Command-and-control leadership is based on the assumption that people are basically lazy, unmotivated and in need of constant supervision. They have to be told what to do and how to do it, either by specialists or by people who are smarter and/or more experienced: i.e. the people who have all the answers. Over time, the assumptions of command-and-control leadership become self-fulfilling prophecies. People become what command-and-control leaders expect them to be. The huge reservoir of intelligence, creativity, good will and energy that other kinds of leaders can liberate from people is unrecognised and wasted.

For a very limited period, in some very unambiguous situations, command-and-control leadership is permissible and can work well. But when it is applied in complex, long-term, open-ended situations, the results can be disastrous. In a fascinating study of its application to environmental and socio-economic problems, C. S. Holling and Gary K. Meffe of the Department of Zoology, University of Florida, tell us: "Attempts to control ecosystems and in socio-economic institutions . . . with more control . . . usually result in unforeseen consequences for both natural ecosystems and human welfare, in the form of collapsing resources, social and economic strife, and losses of biological diversity. . . . If natural levels of variation in system behaviour are reduced through command-and-control, the system becomes less resilient to external perturbations, resulting in crises and surprises." [102]

And in *System Failure*, Jake Chapman reports the consequences of command-and-control leaders applying hard-systems thinking to the 'wicked' problems involved in the delivery of the UK's health services:

1.   The interventions have unintended consequences. The assumptions on which they were based were simply not valid.

2.   Delivery targets are trumpeted but not met.

3.   Key people responsible for the delivery of the system's outputs (doctors, nurses, technicians, clerks, middle managers) experience increasing interference and stress. Top managers are increasingly impatient, punitive and frustrated.

4.   The system loses flexibility and is increasingly unable to adapt to external changes. Acrimony and blame erode trust, motivation and initiative.[103]

To the people trying to make the system work, and in the world outside, the system is widely—and correctly—perceived to be getting worse, not better. At the same time, the politicians and top-managers responsible for the initiatives are—again correctly—perceived to be incompetent and self-serving.

In spite of being inappropriate for the resolution of the hugely complex and unprecedented problems now facing local communities, nations, regions and the whole human family, with very few exceptions command-and-control leadership is still the basic leadership style of all Western 'democracies' and of much of the corporate world.

Command-and-control leadership ensures that the Global Monetocracy continues to respond to the challenges of the 21st century with the same 'tame' solutions—more trade, more deregulation, wars to control essential supplies, competition between states to attract inward investment etc.—that were responsible for creating the situation we are in. It is also fundamentally at odds with the concept of self-organising systems. One of the key innovations in Gaian democracies will be the replacement of command-and-control leaders with liberating leaders, as described in Chapter 5.

Component 3: The 'elite consensus'

The elite consensus upholding the values and assumptions of the Monetocracy

The elite consensus sets limits on the behaviour of everyone in the system. These limits cannot be questioned: they define the paradigm. Anyone who seeks to question any of these propositions will be told that they are not living in the real world.

It is the elite consensus that explains why political, media and business leaders are deaf to warning signs and suggestions for remedial action. Those things are outside their paradigm, their worldview.

There have been many studies of the components of the world-view that underpins the elite consensus.[104] Some of the key points are shown in the box opposite.

Once these presuppositions and principles have been internalised, they become an integral part of the worldview of politicians, bankers, corporate executives, academics, editors and journalists. Spirited debate, criticism and learning are allowed only within the boundaries set by the consensus.

Component 4: The global leadership cadre

> **The global leadership cadre** covering politics, finance, business, academia and the media.

The expenditure of billions of dollars on developing and promoting the theory of neo-liberal economics has been matched by an equally well-funded programme of education and brainwashing to create the elite cadre of Western political leaders. Over the past fifty years, a lavish assortment of study trips, scholarships and 'fellowships', paid for by the U.S. Government and free-market foundations, has been used to groom thousands of politically ambitious young Europeans, Asians, Africans and Latin Americans.

To get a glimpse of how the global leadership cadre is recruited, log-on to *www.cylc.org/alumni/spotlight.html*. There you will find the fond reminiscences of a young Englishman who attended a National Young Leaders Conference while still in school. He recalls "the inspiration that NYLC provided", his "privileged access to Congress and the Supreme Court, as well as to many of the people who work inside government", which had enabled him to "understand and appreciate the value of genuine representative democracy—something we seem to lack in the UK". He hopes to represent people in his future career.

The Elite Consensus

States
- Each country is first and foremost a competitor in the global market and should act according to its own interests.
- All states have a right to use all resources within their reach.

State governments
- Are the ultimate source of civil order.
- Should keep out of the markets.
- Should encourage transnational companies to play a full part in all national and international decisions affecting global trade and development.

Representative democracy
- Is the nearest approach to an ideal democracy that is practicable in the real world and is the true guardian of a free society.

Science and technology
- We can ignore the 'doom-mongers' because science and technology will always find solutions to the problems that worry them.

The market economy
- All human needs express themselves in the market place in monetary terms and therefore the market will lead to optimal solutions for all problems.
- Permanent economic growth is desirable and necessary, with no inherent environmental or human limits to the conversion of life into saleable commodities.
- Individual consumer desires are permanently increasing, unlimited and good.
- Those who do not or cannot express themselves in the competitive process are a problem, but not one that calls for radical reflection.
- The great majority who have only their labour to sell must do so.
- Ever larger transnational corporations are perfectly natural.

Market forces
- Competition is the dominant principle governing relationships of all kinds.
- Freedom to buy and sell in money exchanges is the basis of human liberty and justice.
- Profit maximisation is the engine of social well-being and is not to be hedged by public regulation or ownership.

Private property
- Is good in all things.
- Information is a proprietary and marketable good and a legitimate means for acquiring wealth, power and privilege.

Aggressive individualism
- On the part of individuals, companies and states is acceptable.

This ambitious young man is following in some very big footsteps. Bright and politically ambitious young Britons who have benefited from similarly privileged experiences are now leading members of New Labour in the UK, including the Prime Minister, the Chancellor of the Exchequer and their chief advisers. All, together with Tony Blair's Chief of Staff, Jonathan Powell, are supporters of the British-American Project for the Successor Generation (BAP). The BAP is a little-known but highly influential transatlantic network of 'chosen' politicians, journalists and academics. Regular attendees at BAP meetings are defence and security specialists, NATO advisers, Defence Ministry think-tank people and counter-insurgency experts.

The BAP is funded by the Pew Charitable Trusts of Philadelphia (established in 1985 by the billionaire J. Howard Pew, a devoted supporter of the Republican Party), the far-right Heritage Foundation and the Manhattan Institute for Policy Research (founded by former CIA head William Casey). It organises regular meetings of "24 Americans and 24 Britons aged between 28 and 40 who . . . would be leaders in their country and perhaps internationally". As Nick Cohen noted in the *Observer* of 31 October 1999: "The Brits are encouraged to help their careers by following the American way." In its 1997 newsletter, following New Labour's election victory, BAP warmly welcomed the elevation of its members to the Blair Cabinet: "Congratulations from all of us!"

Apart from politicians and trade unionists, the ranks of the Atlanticist elite include Charles Moore, the editor of the *Daily Telegraph*, James Naughtie, formerly of the *Guardian* and now presenting Radio 4's *Today* programme, and Trevor Phillips, a former-TV reporter who is now Chair of the Commission for Racial Equality.

The readiness with which ambitious British politicians and journalists embrace the values and policies of their American friends is the fruit of years of relentless conditioning by the combined forces of the US State Department, the Central Intelligence Agency, right-wing think-tanks, the British Foreign Office and the British intelligence services. After World War II hundreds of millions of dollars were lavished on travel, scholarships, hospitality and propaganda to counter the ideological influence of communism. This strategy, combined with revulsion at the appalling excesses of Soviet and Chinese communism, resulted in generations of Europe's nominally left-wing politicians, trade unionists, journalists, artists and academics becoming fervently anti-communist in public, and, more importantly, enthusiastic devotees of free-market capitalism in private.

The New Labour project is evidence of the triumph of this policy. The slavish adherence to neo-liberal economic theory and the elite consensus on globalisation are only the most visible signs of this triumph. Much less obvious is the way in which every aspect of UK government is now dominated by the interests of big business. For nearly 60 years, US free-market ideologues have financed, educated, employed and smoothed the career-paths of an increasing number of the members of the front bench of the British Labour Party (and Social Democrats from every other major nation), whether in government or in opposition. The consequence is that, in 2003, when Washington says jump, the response from their chosen placemen in our nominally British government is to ask "How high?"

Component 5: The working partnership

The big business–government partnership
(with big business as the lead partner)

A close working partnership between the governments of the Western 'democracies' and big business is both a natural consequence of the Global Monetocracy's purpose and the obvious strategy for implementing it.

As evidence of the nature of the partnership, the membership of President George W. Bush's cabinet is perhaps the most blatant example.[105] Tony Blair has followed the US model, by including several millionaire businessmen in his New Labour government. He appointed as head of his government's energy tax review team the former chairman of British Airways, Lord Marshall, who had lobbied against proposals to tax aviation fuel. He persuaded the G8 summit to elect as head of its global task force on renewable energy the Chairman of Shell, a company doing its utmost to increase sales of fossil fuels.[106] He appointed the chairman of Northern Foods, Lord Haskins, as 'rural recovery coordinator'.[107] And he took with him to the World Summit in Johannesburg the chief executives of three multinationals that had been involved in rows over important wildlife habitats and ignoring human rights.[108]

Less obviously, in the wake of the BSE and foot and mouth crises, the UK Government set up the Curry Commission to advise on the future of farming and food, but the terms of reference, insisting that the Commission's advice must be "consistent with the Government's aims . . . for increased trade liberalisation", could not be questioned. Even less obvious from the outside is the degree to which big business takes a central role in detailed policy-making and implementation alongside the civil service. The British Government has 320 Task Forces with over 2500 members. Big business takes about 900 of those seats, compared with a mere 70 Trade Union representatives. To see the detailed picture of how the Task Forces work log-on to *www.red-star-research.org.uk*.

In *Captive State*, George Monbiot has described the government-backed corporate take-over of public services in the UK. In a *Guardian* article he wrote: "State and corporate power are fusing almost everywhere on earth, but in Italy they have condensed into the stocky figure of a single man. Silvio Berlusconi, the prime minister, is worth around $10 billion. . . . His control of most of the private media (through his businesses) and most of the public media (through the government) means that he can exercise a dominion unprecedented in a democratic nation over the thoughts and feelings of his people."[109] After their recent meeting, Berlusconi was reported as telling the press that he and Blair saw eye-to-eye "on all the matters that were raised".[110] Elsewhere in the world we can see that in the newly 'democratised' republics of the former USSR the line between Government, big business and organised crime is so blurred as to be indistinguishable.

The effect on democratic politics of such cosy unanimity between government and big business is disastrous. As subscriptions from members and trade unions decline, politicians and parties become ever more reliant on donations from wealthy businessmen and large corporations to pay for the elaborate machinery of electoral success—pollsters, focus groups, advertising and so on. The pay-off for the corporate funders is that, in return, taxpayers contribute massively to the little discussed 'corporate welfare system'.

'Corporate welfare' takes many forms: from tax-breaks, legislation and the provision of infrastructure (roads, schools, local government services etc.) to the pernicious practice of handing over licences for patents arising from Government-financed research. Then there are the straightforward subsidies paid out by governments to businesses, totalling $1,900 billion per year worldwide, of which $1,450 billion are reckoned to be perverse subsidies—those that severely distort the global economy and inflict massive injuries on the environment.[111] The lobbying power of the organisations representing subsidised industries can be gauged from the fact that, while only $50 billion per annum is spent on aid globally, $350 billion per annum is spent on subsidies to agribusiness alone.

The armed forces and other arms of the state are frequently used by governments to serve the interests of big business abroad. There are clear links, for example, between the dependence of big business on fossil fuels and government action abroad, most notably that of the United States. The US produces less than half the petroleum it uses and thus a prime aim of its foreign policy is to secure outside sources. The drive for US military and economic domination, the war on Afghanistan and its aim of controlling Iraq are closely linked to its wish to secure sources of oil in the Middle East and Central Asia.[112]

Another pay-off for political donations is the huge effort governments make to ensure that the regulation of state and international economic activity and laws relating, for example, to patents, are 'business-friendly'. This factor generally trumps environmental or safety considerations. According to Mae-Wan Ho, many of the dangers of genetic engineering have not been taken on board by the regulatory bodies. "On the contrary, safety regulations have been notably relaxed. The public is being used, against their will, as guinea pigs for genetically engineered products."[113]

Governments serve big business in more subtle ways, by standing up for the Global Monetocracy's purpose and not allowing the democratic process to be used to question the elite consensus. Politicians consistently use the authority vested in them as elected representatives, plus all their political skills and the state's communication systems, to assert and confirm the elite's values as being—beyond question—in the public interest, whatever the indications to the contrary. In a recent interview, Kevin Phillips, formerly chief political strategist for President Richard Nixon stated that money has "taken control of both parties [i.e. Republicans and Democrats], pretty much taken control of the culture and controls the whole dynamic of politics". Their own dependence on corporate donations explained why the Democrats had held back from commenting on connections between Enron and the Bush family "partly because they're so interested in raising money that they can't see their soul in the mirror".[114]

The Carlyle Group perfectly demonstrates the partnership between big business and government. Established in 1987 and based in Washington DC, it specialises in buying up companies with government contracts. Its rapid success, according to the Group's website, is based on a 'worldwide network of investment professionals who can capitalize on one another's expertise in specific industries . . . [which] opens investment opportunities that would otherwise not be available or identifiable. . . .'

The names of those 'investment professionals' include: former US President George Bush Sr.; James Baker, Secretary of State under Bush Sr.; Frank Carlucci, Secretary of Defense under Ronald Reagan; and John Major, the former British Prime Minister.

With a roll call like this, it's not surprising that concerns have been raised about the political influence wielded by the company. For example, Carlyle is the US's eleventh largest defence contractor: decisions taken by George Bush Jr. could directly influence the size of his father's pay packet. And questions were asked when Donald Rumsfeld—current US Secretary of Defense, and former college wrestling partner of Carlucci—awarded an $11 billion contract for the Crusader tank, widely criticised as a Cold War relic, to a company owned by Carlyle. That the Bin Laden family were once investors in the firm has only added to the sense of unease.

Component 6: The armoury of operational instruments
The Global Monetocracy implements its purpose by means of a huge range of 'operational instruments'. These are the external manifestations of the Global Monetocracy at work in the world, at any one time.

As we saw in Chapter 1, purposeful human systems have the capacity to adapt to changes in their environments. The Global Monetocracy is no exception. Its operational instruments can change without affecting the fundamentals of the system. For example, in the last half-century, transnational corporate globalisation has replaced imperialism and colonialism as the mechanism for delivering global economic growth. Thus, even if any of these instruments, or several of them, were reformed, the Global Monetocracy would carry on. It would find other ways of implementing its purpose, just as·it has substituted globalisation for colonialism.

As these operating instruments are the means for delivering the Global Monetocracy's purpose, it is **their** effects that people—and the environment—immediately experience. As such, it is not surprising that each of these instruments has attracted much analysis, criticism and opposition. Environmental, human-rights and community campaigners have succeeded in making some small inroads into particular aspects of their operations. But overall, unless the whole Global Monetocracy system is reconfigured, calls to change, or even to abolish, one or more of these instruments will not have a lasting impact on the Global Monetocracy as a whole. The other side of that coin is that, as the Global Monetocracy is reconfigured, each of these instruments can be modified or scrapped. Nothing is set in stone. They are all man-made, created by governments and parliaments elected through representative democracy. They can all be unmade or fundamentally reconfigured; and, through a global network of Gaian democracies, many of them will be.

It is far beyond the scope of this Briefing to attempt to present a comprehensive account of the Monetocracy's operational instruments. For amplification of our very brief comments, please see *www.wwdemocracy.org*.

- **Operational Instruments 1: Transnational corporate capitalism.** It is frequently pointed out that corporations now dominate governments throughout the world, at the expense of democracy. This misses the real point, which is that 'ownership' of the Global Monetocracy rests with an international elite who effectively control both the corporations and the governments. Their purpose is economic growth for their own benefit, and, provided

FIGURE 3. Component 6: The armoury of operational instruments

National policies and state agencies
interest rates, tax systems, trade liberalisation, free movement of capital across state boundaries, arms sales, corporate welfare, privatisation of public services, export guarantees, tied aid, limiting workers' rights, de-regulation, 'competition', sustainable development, national 'security', Treasury and Defence ministries and foreign services

Financial and legal instruments
debt-money, reserve currencies, property law, corporate law and patent law

Opinion formation
official propaganda and corporate public relations, political campaigns and elections, advertising, foreign 'bogey-men', state security apparatus, education, selective news coverage, free-market foundations and think-tanks

Transnational corporate capitalism
owning and controlling the entire financial system, defining work, entertainment, transport, consumerist culture, taking over all public services, industrialised agriculture and fishing, taking over the commons, political corruption, corporate control of global mass media

International agencies and treaties
International Monetary Fund (IMF), World Trade Organisation (WTO), World Bank, EU, World Economic Forum (WEF), Transatlantic Business Forum (TABF), North American and other regional 'Free-Trade Areas', European Round Table of Industrialists

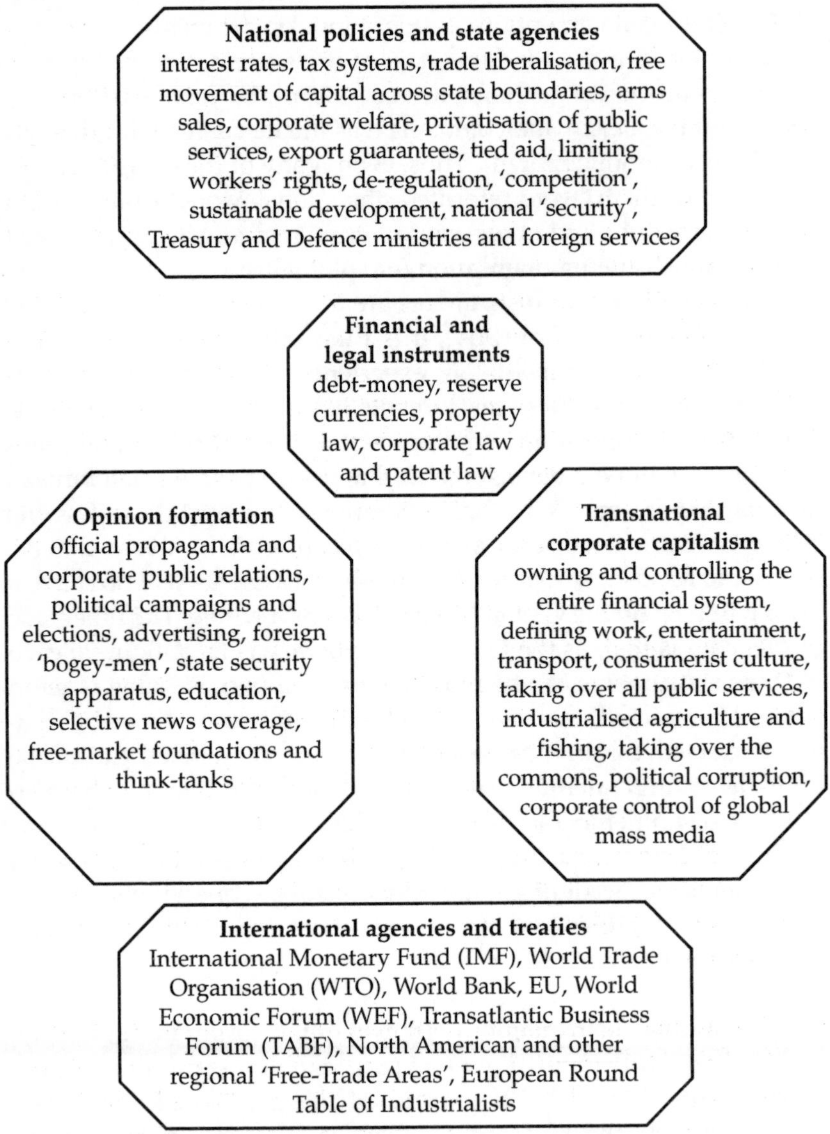

For convenience, Figure 3 represents the main components of the operational instruments as separate and 2-dimensional, but in the real world they are nested in a multi-dimensional cluster, interconnected and interacting.

the Global Monetocracy is delivering this—which as we have seen is precisely what it is designed to do—it matters not what the relative position of corporations and governments happens to be.

The text on *www.wwdemocracy.org* explains why the corporation is the ideal legal structure for implementing the Global Monetocracy's purpose. A vast web of financial institutions provides the machinery that enables people to make money out of money and, crucially, enables the global leadership cadre to exercise the power of money over the real economies of the real world.

Looked at from the point of view of Gaian systems, all we see is a string of breaches of the rules for sustainable systems: the disconnection between the investors, market traders and executives and the people who are affected by their decisions and actions. There is no chain of interdependency, no partnership; there are no feedback mechanisms to ensure that their operations are not destroying the global environment.

- **Operational Instruments 2: Financial and legal instruments.** We have already discussed debt-money and reserve currencies in the section on the Global Monetocracy's purpose at the beginning of this chapter. The field of property, corporate and patent laws is vast. The adverse impact of these laws on communities, biodiversity and other natural resources is well documented. The only point we need to highlight here is that this entire world of laws, largely made by parliaments, has been created within the value programme of the elite consensus, and in accordance with the operational theories of the Global Monetocracy. They are all part of the larger picture. As long as that overarching system remains in force there is no chance of serious reform.

- **Operational Instruments 3: National policies.** Once we see governments as supporting players in the larger project of the Global Monetocracy, it is obvious why policies like privatisation and globalisation are non-negotiable. They enable the money economy to keep expanding. As a result, overwhelming evidence of their inefficiency and adverse social impacts has to be totally disregarded.

- **Operational Instruments 4: International agencies and treaties.**
  Governments and big business work together on the democracy-free international stage through a complex set of agencies and treaties. Some of the most important are shown in Figure 3. They are all controlled by members of the global leadership cadre, they all operate within the elite consensus and they are all dedicated to the Global Monetocracy's purpose and the agenda of economic and corporate growth that serves the purpose.

  We have already noted that the monopolistic position now enjoyed by neo-liberal economics is no accident, but the successful outcome of a concerted and well-funded programme; and that the mindset of the global leadership cadre is the product of an equally determined programme of indoctrination. There is a similar story of deliberately organised activity initiated and dominated by the corporate elite, to explain the workings of international corporate capitalism.

  Many people are familiar with the appallingly destructive operations of the better-known agencies like the World Bank, the International Monetary Fund (IMF) and the World Trade Organisation (WTO). But these are only the tip of the iceberg. Radical commentators such as Susan George, Robin Ramsay and Vandana Shiva, and groups such as the London-based World Development Movement, have documented a global network of organisations tailor-made to promote corporate capitalism. The immensely influential World Economic Forum (WEF), for example, brings together two thousand corporate executives, politicians and academics at its annual meeting, traditionally held in Davos, Switzerland. *New Internationalist* quotes the WEF veteran Samuel P. Huntingdon as saying, "Davos people control virtually all international institutions, many of the world's governments and the bulk of the world's economic and military capabilities."

- **Operational Instruments 5: Opinion moulding**
  The text on *www.wwdemocracy.org* illustrates the unscrupulous use politicians and big business make of all forms of media and advertising to further their ends. Opinion moulding has become the prime skill of both partners in the big business-government coalition.

Conclusion

Now that we have a rough outline of the Global Monetocracy as a single system, we are able to recognise the problems set out in Chapter Two as examples of the system's emergent properties.

We can also see that the Global Monetocracy, when looked at as a whole, is an incompetent system—incompetent to co-exist with Gaia, which is what humans must learn to do if we are to survive. If you have the wrong system, there is no way of doing the right thing with it. However clever the president may be, however expertly advised the chief finance minister or central bank manager—the better they do their jobs, the worse the outcome is bound to be. It is the complete paradigm that is failing us, because it is systemically incompetent to handle the complex needs of human societies and their relations with Gaia. While we have Global Monetocracy, rather than a global network of Gaian democracies, we are doomed. Nothing short of a remodelling of the entire economic/political system can save us.

Now that we have identified the main components of the Global Monetocracy we can better understand its true nature. We can see how, on the one hand, the Global Monetocracy is a complex, adaptive, self-organising system, simply because that is the nature of any large purposeful human system. Its self-organising character takes the form, for example, of conflict between countries, and competition between corporations and amongst the elite. We have already noted the system's capacity to adapt to changing circumstances. Yet, while it has this complex, adaptive, self-organising character, the Global Monetocracy as a whole is also locked into its purpose of economic growth; and the culture of command-and-control pervades government throughout the system.

Finally, we can see why people have lost faith in 'democracy'. We no longer believe in Athena, the goddess of citizenship. Politicians are held in low esteem. A complete failure of democracy is staring us in the face. The less faith we have in governments, the less responsibility we give them, and a devastating reinforcement feedback process is underway. In the resulting vacuum, the sway of 'market forces' inevitably increases. The sheer incompetence of government by command-and-control has encouraged the idea that government's main job is to reduce the scope of government and increase the freedom of the corporations; and this is now successfully promoted as a vote winner for candidates for high office. We will leave the last words of Chapter 3 to William E. Rees, of the University of British Columbia:

> "In recent years the governing elites of the market democracies have persuaded or cajoled virtually the entire world to adopt a common myth of uncommon power. All major national governments and mainstream international agencies are united in a vision of global development and poverty alleviation centred on unlimited economic expansion fuelled by open markets and more liberalized trade.

> "For the first time, the world seems to be converging on a common development ideology, one that promises ever-increasing wealth for everyone, everywhere. The downside is that constant repetition of the myth has so conditioned the population that the majority seems incapable of applying basic rules of evidence to the growing cascade of data that refute it."[115]

Chapter 4
A Political Vacuum

The resilience of the system

The resilience of the Global Monetocracy is understandable when we see it as a complex purposeful adaptive system. All such systems can withstand a great deal of buffeting, bruising and wounding without seriously affecting their overarching character. The system will respond, but only in ways that enable it to pursue its goals. Changes in some of the Global Monetocracy's operative functions are thus possible, provided the changes do not affect its purpose. Even if parts of the Global Monetocracy are successfully reformed, the onward momentum of the system as a whole will not be affected.

In the case of the Global Monetocracy, the value program embedded in the elite consensus hides from all those within its thrall both the truth about the incompetence of the regime and the dangers that lie ahead. Although we have a global suicide economy, the elite mindset will blindly resist change. The power of the elite consensus is such that any challenge to the Global Monetocracy is experienced by members of the elite as a personal attack and is resisted accordingly. There is immense pressure on individuals to close ranks and conform.

In response to the overwhelming power of the Global Monetocracy even the most knowledgeable and concerned citizens are tempted to limit their civic horizons to their friends, families, work and the communities of place and interest to which they belong. This is where their skills and creativity can flourish, where they can be of some use. They may well actively support some of the vast number of charitable organisations engaged in nursing the wounds inflicted by the regime on individuals, communities and ecosystems—but taking part in politics is out of the question. Clearly, as long as a substantial proportion of citizens are politically inactive, they present no threat to the Global Monetocracy. In effect they are following the lead of many of the Global Monetocracy's most prominent critics and opponents. They either they try to work with and within the system, or they engage in localised or single-issue campaigns of resistance and defence, rather than taking the political route to fundamental systems change.

Working with and within the system

Working with and within the Global Monetocracy stands no chance of achieving the scale and totality of change that humanity's global predicament demands. It is a non-negotiable condition of engagement with the Global Monetocracy that, in effect, everyone—environmentalists, civil rights activists, politicians, civil servants, professionals, academics, consultants—has to sign up to the 'elite consensus' we outlined in Chapter 3.

Many politicians are very well aware of the trends we referred to in Chapter 2. An example is the UK's Minister of Environment, Michael Meacher. Few public figures have done more to expose and publicise the facts. Yet he is a loyal upholder of the Global Monetocracy's purpose, as this quotation from a recent speech shows: "If we are expecting, indeed encouraging, the developing world to grow economically in order to eradicate poverty, we need to lead the way in decoupling growth from environmental degradation. . . . We need to find ways of channelling private sector investment into many of the poorer developing countries." Growth and more—private sector—growth!

In the UK the New Labour government is continuously spawning new programmes to alleviate the ill effects of the Global Monetocracy. Its Neighbourhood Renewal Programme, intended to address the "the problems of areas of multiple deprivation" is perhaps the most enlightened. But it in no way threatens the Global Monetocracy that caused these problems in the first place. The deprived areas themselves are not really the problem: the real problem is the Global Monetocracy. The programme cannot begin to reduce poverty, reinvent democracy or address the disconnection between humanity and the rest of the Gaian system. Those 'wicked' problems lie at the root of the dysfunctional nature of the system as a whole.

On the international scene the main programme intended to address the effects of economic growth is the 1997 Kyoto protocol on reducing greenhouse gases. But the climate change negotiations have been heavily influenced by the corporate sector.[116] And the market mechanisms and loopholes finally agreed at Marrakech in November 2001 are considered to render the whole process essentially worthless.[117] It seems unlikely to have any significant effect on restraining economic growth.

Far more subtly, the elite consensus restricts the perceptions of the most outspoken critics of current policies. An outstanding example on the global stage is Joseph Stiglitz, former Chief Economist to the World Bank, whose recent book *Globalization and its Discontents* is a scathing exposure of the disastrous effects of globalisation as currently conducted.[118] It even includes a generous acknowledgement of the part played by anti-globalisation protesters in bringing these effects to light. The book contains, however, no recognition of the systemic incompetence of the Global Monetocracy. Growth is not the issue. Rather, "The question has to do with particular policies." For Stiglitz, what matters is "making sure that democratic decisions are made means ensuring that a broad range of economists, officials and experts from developing countries are actively involved in the debate." No room for 'the bewildered herd' at the Stiglitz debate. Instead we see that Walter Lippman's notion of democracy as a kind of exclusive club is built into the thinking of one of the most effective critics of the policies of the Global Monetocracy.

Another popular tactic is to work with the corporate sector in the hope of getting multinational corporations to respond responsibly to the ethical and sustainability challenges of today. Within the last few decades, many corporations have voluntarily adopted one of the available ethical or sustainability codes, for example ISO 14001. But even if they all adopted and abided by these codes, which is extremely unlikely, the systemic features of the Global Monetocracy would remain unchanged.

As a means of bringing about radical change of the kind we know to be crucially necessary, this entire agenda of reform from within is misconceived. It is attempting the impossible: it can only serve to prolong the life of the Global Monetocracy, by lulling the public into thinking there is a possibility that capitalist corporations could behave responsibly within the current system. This agenda assumes that the Global Monetocracy is reasonable, and interested in justice and sustainability. It is not. Given its purpose, it cannot be.

The Civil Society Movement (CSM)

Through its participation in the World Social Forums in Porto Alegre, Brazil, the CSM has undoubtedly provided a much-needed sense of hope that "another world is possible". However, the evidence shows that the CSM is not, and will never be, capable of achieving such an admirable aim. The background is as follows.

After the global economic crash of the 1930s, the forces that drive the Global Monetocracy were somewhat in retreat. But as we outlined in Chapter 3, from 1945 onwards, with the unstinting support of numerous right-wing think-tanks, Wall Street, the City of London, and institutions such as the IMF and the World Bank, 'laissez-faire' made a spectacular comeback in the form of neo-liberal economics. In the last twenty years of the 20th century the Global Monetocracy scored victory after victory.

In 1979 Margaret Thatcher gained power in the UK, and in 1980 Ronald Reagan became President of the USA. Thatcher and Reagan appointed neo-liberal zealots as Cabinet members and policy advisers. Their example was followed in Australia and New Zealand, Canada and Western Europe. For the first time in fifty years, Western 'democracies' had governments that purposefully set out to create the conditions in which the gap between the rich and the rest of us got wider and wider. "Greed is good for you!" became the mantra of the corporate, media and political elites. According to *Business Week* magazine, in 1980 the average chief executive of a large corporation in the USA was paid 42 times as much as the average worker; by 2000 it was 531 times as much.[119] Executive-worker pay differentials in the UK and Europe followed the same pattern between 1980 and 2002.

When the Berlin Wall came down in 1990 and the Soviet empire collapsed, the Cold War was over. Capitalism had triumphed over Communism without a shot being fired in Europe. By the beginning of the 1990s, the only opponents to the onward march of the corporations were the increasingly well-organised environmental and human rights campaigners, now known collectively as the 'Civil Society Movement' or 'Civil Society'.

The Global Monetocracy's strategy was simple. While Governments and international agencies lent a more or less sympathetic ear to the CSM's appeals for funds and consultation, they pushed ahead as quickly as possible with the implementation of policies to remove any remaining barriers to the corporate dominance of the global environment, economy and community: 'economic globalisation' had arrived.

For a while the global CSM was more or less fooled. During the early 1990s, they came to the UN Conference on Environment and Development in Rio de Janeiro with some hopes of success, as did the scientists and environmental NGOs who attended the UN's Kyoto Conference on Climate Change in 1997. In each case they had to sit by helplessly while the governments of the major economic powers supported the manipulation of the agendas and outcomes by the hugely influential lobbyists of the corporate public relations industry.

Gradually, however, the full import of the Global Monetocracy's project began to become much clearer. The replacement of the General Agreement on Tariffs and Trade (GATT) with the even more corporate-friendly World Trade Organisation provoked only muted resistance. But the attempt to introduce the Multilateral Agreement on Investments (MAI), which would have massively privileged corporations over sovereign states, precipitated stiff opposition not only from the CSM but also from local government. The Federation of Canadian Municipalities, for example, pointed out that ". . . any government bound by the MAI shall 'not expropriate or nationalize directly or indirectly an investment in its territory of an investor . . . or take any measure or measures having equivalent effect', thereby putting in question the ability of municipalities and regional districts, acting in the public interest, to limit the use of property through zoning."[120] The Federation petitioned the Canadian Prime Minister to demand a "permanent and explicit exemption in the Agreement, limiting its application to areas of federal jurisdiction". The CSM mounted an unprecedented global resistance campaign via the internet, and their combined forces managed to stop the MAI in its tracks—at least temporarily.

After the success of anti-MAI campaign, in rapid succession there then came the anti-globalisation protests at the WTO meeting in Seattle in 1999, at the 2001 G8 Summit in Genoa and at a number of other gatherings of the Global Monetocracy elite. Out of the dust of these events emerged the shining beacon of the 2001 and 2002 World Social Forums. These brought together every strand of the global Civil Society in Porto Alegre, Brazil.

Thus, by September 2002, when the UN's Johannesburg Summit on the environment came around, the likely scenario was pretty well accepted in advance. As with all previous summits, on whatever aspect of the global problematique—the environment, trade, poverty, population—the transnational corporations and their political place-persons would flex their muscles and once again outmanoeuvre Civil Society. The CSM would do its best to resist the Global Monetocracy on behalf of Gaia and the billions of impoverished and dispossessed people around the world, but the outcomes would be what Barry Coates, of the London-based World Development Movement,[121] has called a "roll over"; they would ensure the continued expansion the debt-based global economy.

It was against this background that thousands of Civil Society delegates descended on Johannesburg in September 2002 for the World Summit on Sustainable Development. They attended with little expectation of any substantive progress, but at least there was a chance to strengthen resistance and defence networks—and to protest on behalf of the human family and the natural world against the Global Monetocracy.

By contrast, at the World Social Forums in Porto Alegre there is an abundance of hope and optimism. The aim of every one of the tens of thousands of delegates is to take significant steps towards building a different world. Nothing less is envisaged by the men and women who represent the major NGOs that form the CSM. The question is: how realistic is their hope of doing so?

Defence vs Change strategies

During the 1990s the USA, the UK, the Commonwealth, the EU, the UN and many leading foundations funded and promoted the NGOs that make up the CSM. With the approval of these supporters, the CSM puts forward the idea of a global democratic movement as a means of providing nothing less than an alternative form of **global democracy**. According to David Callahan, a Fellow of the Century Fund, New York, the aims of the CSM are to:

- Bring citizens of many nations into creative democratic communion.

- Increase social responsiveness and democratic accountability of over-powerful governments.

- Control the power of transnational corporate capitalism.[122]

Within that framework there lurks a dream that, as Callahan says, "some day a single set of political, social and economic norms will bind all the planet's people together in a more just and democratic fashion." However, beneath the 'democratic' rhetoric the CSM is actually engaged in a project through which a global coalition of unelected non-governmental agencies, plus the United Nations, can eventually prove to be an effective vehicle for constraining rogue governments and regulating global capital. They aim to re-distribute assets and opportunities, inject social values into market processes and hold economic institutions to account for their actions.

That said, there is no doubt that the idealism, dedication and creativity of the people and organisations within the CSM have brought hope and meaning to millions of the most disadvantaged people around the world. Without their work the world would be a much poorer place. For thousands of campaigns all over the world, the CSM, although partially funded by multinational corporations, rightly deserves the respect and gratitude of every thoughtful person—no matter where their funding comes from.

However, in seeking to extend its role to providing an apparently apolitical form of global democracy, the CSM seems to be ignoring the political realities that have confronted them so many times. Supporters of the CSM believe that a bandwagon of historical transformation is now rolling, whereas the brutal truth is that whenever they have tried to take on the Global Monetocracy over major social, economic or environmental issues they have been 'rolled over', as Barry Coates said after the 2001 WTO summit at Doha.

Even with the backing of the United Nations, when it comes to the global and national issues—as distinct from local skirmishes and the occasional big battle—a coalition of NGOs is no threat to the coalition of nation states, transnational corporations and financial institutions in charge of the Global Monetocracy.

Moreover, even if they had the clout, on what kind of political authority would they conduct the struggle? Distinguished, honourable and able as they are, the leaders of the CSM have no political or constitutional legitimacy. They have no popular mandate; they have not placed their ideas and characters before the bar of public scrutiny.

Thus, the whole question of their political engagement or disengagement presents the CSM with profound difficulties. From our perspective, there is also a fundamental strategic reason why the Civil Society's global democracy project is fatally flawed. Their 'change strategy' is in fact a 'defence strategy'. We pointed out in the Summary and Introduction that the difference is absolutely crucial, and illustrated it with George Lakey's account of the disillusionment felt in the aftermath of the defeated Russian coup.

The point cannot be emphasised strongly enough. George Lakey persuaded the young Russians that if they wanted to bring about fundamental change they would have to mobilise a new popular political movement, contest elections and win power. Nowhere in the CSM's strategy is there any mention of the need for active **political** engagement or the mobilisation of political people-power in order to bring about 'another world'. There is no discussion of even the possibility of founding powerful new political parties, fighting elections, winning office and forming governments with a mandate for fundamental economic and social change. Instead—perhaps as a condition of their funding—they have abandoned the political arena to the Global Monetocracy and limited their basic orientation towards a wide range of defence and resistance strategies while proclaiming that they are striving to bring about 'another world'. The truth is that, vitally important as it is, social defence can never be a substitute for fundamental **political** change. Somehow, the two strands have to be integrated into a coherent, multi-faceted global strategy—and that can only happen within a systems perspective.

Chapter 5
Gaian Democracy

"We are dealing with . . . a systemically interdependent global community. It is this level of [reality] which we must keep before our eyes if we are able to inspire action designed to assure our collective and hence our individual survival."—Ludwig von Bertalanffy, pioneer systems scientist.

Giving 'democracy' a new meaning

From the outset of our work leading to this Briefing it became clear that if the concept of 'sustainable societies' was to have any real meaning, its primary orientation had to be ecological. We then had the task of integrating the political, social and economic aspects of the new paradigm with the primary ecological orientation. From here it was a relatively short step to concluding that what we were working on could best be described as a Gaian model of democracy.

The theory of Gaian Democracy should be seen as providing a versatile model that can be adapted to different contexts. It is a systemic framework upon which different societies would be able to build their own Gaian democracies. Thus we have been referring to the model as 'Gaian Democracy' in the singular, but we envisage many networks of Gaian democracies, related to each other on the principle of 'network government' described towards the end of this chapter.

From youthful to mature systems

When new kinds of complex, adaptive, self-organising systems evolve, or are introduced into an environment, they establish themselves by going through a 'youthful' stage of ferocious competition and exponential growth. The youthful stage is essential if the new system is to achieve the condition of viability that enables it to survive in both cooperation and competition with the other systems in

FIGURE 4: The Gaian paradigm of democracy

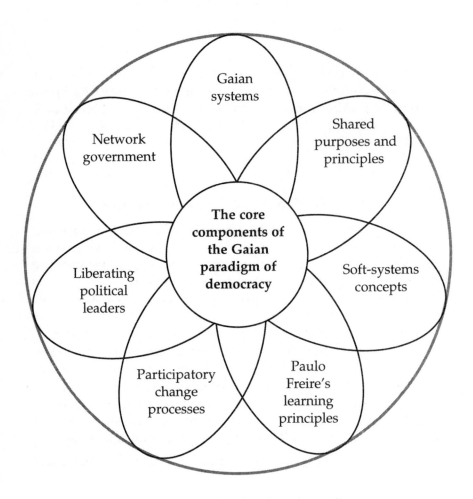

The model has both a political and a systems dimension. Its purpose in political terms is to initiate the co-creation of just and sustainable societies; in systems terms the purpose is to facilitate the purposeful evolution of our societies, from youthful systems pursuing exponential growth to mature systems in a state of dynamic stability in equilibrium with our environment.

its environment. Sooner or later, however, external factors start to limit the system's growth, and it settles down into a 'mature' state of 'dynamic stability' in equilibrium with its environment.

But if we look today at the complex, adaptive, self-organising system we call 'humanity', we see that in spite of having met with the problems described in Chapter 2, its youthful growth stage is being driven ever faster by the Global Monetocracy. Unless we act ourselves, 'humanity' will soon meet the same fate as any other system in a vicious downward spiral mode. If that were to happen, it would be extremely painful for billions of us. Far better, in our view, to use our systems knowledge to consciously evolve from youthful exponential growth to mature dynamic stability.[123] It will not be the end of the 'growth' of human societies, but instead of the growth being **quantitative** through ever more rapacious consumption of our environment, it will become **qualitative** in terms of constantly rising levels of shared understanding and societal learning, through thousands of self-organising Gaian democracies. In this chapter we explain how thinking in terms of the Gaian model of democracy could help us to achieve that transformation through conscious evolution.

Notes on FIGURE 4 (see left)
As with the diagram of the Global Monetocracy, the components of Gaian democracies are shown as separate but overlapping. They cannot be thought of as bits that can be disconnected from the whole. In the diagram we show them in two dimensions and static. In the real world, they will be dynamic, nested, inter-acting, multi-dimensional and constantly evolving as the system as a whole learns and adapts. We will describe the various components in turn, starting with Gaian systems and proceeding clockwise.

It is worth noting that a broad distinction may be made between Gaian systems and network government, and the other five components. For Gaian systems and network government we are relying on the broad systems concepts described in the first few sections of Chapter 1. The other five components are in a different category: they are concerned with the way human systems work and how they can be changed. For these components we need to make use of the soft-systems concepts described in the last section of Chapter 1. The combination of these two strands of systems science is what gives Gaian democracy its power.

The new paradigm

Component 1: Gaia
Key propositions:

- Gaia is a system of interacting biological and material subsystems that have co-evolved together over billions of years and depend on each other.

- Human beings are a species that has evolved like any other species, with all that implies in terms of interdependence, self-organisation and the other characteristics of evolved systems.

- The Gaian system as a whole appears to be approaching one of its periodic system-shifts, a process which our industrial and agricultural activity is accelerating.

It is widely recognised outside the elites of the Global Monetocracy that our industrial and economic systems must be reconfigured to work with natural systems, instead of treating them as an inexhaustible resource. Our human societies must somehow reconnect with nature.

The characteristics of Gaia as a system, and of human beings and human societies as sub-systems of Gaia are deeply significant in relation to democracy. The capacity of Gaian systems to self-organise is the key to their capacity for survival and adaptation. Our democratic systems need to be configured so as to aim towards achieving ordered relationships between the self-organised actions of the members of a particular democratic system, the democracy of which they are a part, and the Gaian system to which we all belong. Many will optimistically agree with James Lovelock's view that, "Potentially, at least, we have the intelligence to learn how to work with Gaia, rather than undermining her."[124] The intelligence? Yes. But systems for co-learning how to use it? No. Under the Global Monetocracy there is no possibility whatsoever of that potential being realised. The only chance, we believe, of averting the disaster that a Gaian system-shift will spell for the human family, is a system-shift in our democracies. In that sense, we are in a race to reconfigure our democratic systems before Gaia launches on her own systems shift. All we can hope is that Gaia does not get there first.

In our current state of knowledge, it is impossible to say whether the Gaian-shift will result in a new ice age, or the melting of the polar ice-caps and the drowning of millions of low-lying islands and coastal cities, towns and villages. It is important to note that the shift is an example of Gaia's balancing feedback mechanisms in operation, and that, because of the phenomena of systems lag, it may now be irreversible. Even if our outputs of carbon dioxide and methane were reduced to preindustrial levels tomorrow, the amounts that we have already added to the atmosphere could be sufficient to trigger a Gaian system-shift. Unfortunately, because of the complex nature of the systems involved, no one can predict when the shift, if it occurs, will happen. When it does come it will happen quickly, in a matter of decades. At that time, if the human family has reconfigured its societies into Gaian democracies, their chances of adapting speedily and creatively to the new Gaian environment will be vastly improved. If today's Global Monetocracy still holds sway, the consequences of the Gaian shift are likely to be horrific.

Component 2: Shared purposes and principles
Key propositions (see also Chapter 1):

- Gaian democracies will only become increasingly just and sustainable if their citizens understand, are committed to, and share, a set of purposes and moral and ecological principles.

- Purpose and principles cannot be handed down from above. They must be developed through intensive participative processes.

- Plans, programmes and policies are meaningless unless they have been derived from a shared set of purposes and the principles.

As we saw in Chapter 3, the value program of the elite consensus ensures that the Global Monetocracy's purpose is presented as an inevitable fact of life. In Gaian democracies, citizens will arrive at and frequently review their purposes and principles through intensive participative processes. In doing so, they will gain a shared understanding of the relevance of purpose and principles to every aspect of their societies.

Purpose and principles constitute what Dee Hock calls the 'genetic code' of a purposeful human system.[125] They bind the community together. It is against them that all decisions and acts will be judged. Moreover, he says, "A compelling purpose, and powerful beliefs about conduct in pursuit of it, seemed to me infinitely more sensible and robust than mechanical plans, detailed objectives and predetermined outcomes." We profoundly agree with Dee Hock when he also declares: "Without a deeply held, commonly shared purpose that gives meaning to their lives; without deeply held, commonly shared, ethical values and beliefs about conduct in pursuit of purpose that all may trust and rely upon, communities steadily disintegrate, and organizations progressively become instruments of tyranny. This isn't a bunch of platitudes, but a manifesto of what the people in the organization believe in and care about in their gut. And getting there is going to be downright excruciating. . . . What we're trying to do is build a community. And it's only when that community has solid agreement on purposes and principles that you can start talking about the concept and structure of the organization."

Because it can take some time to arrive at a shared understanding of the purposes and principles of the reconfigured system, the difficult task of working them out may arouse deep impatience. It is all too easy to by-pass this stage in the reconfiguring process in order to commit our valuable time, energy and resources to **actually doing something** about the host of chronic problems that cry out for urgent attention. The main reasons why this stage is so significant are these:

- As we work towards increased understanding and a greater sense of shared purposes and principles, we gain a growing awareness of the web of interdependencies within the system, and between it and its environment—a greater understanding of the way the whole system works, and of our part in it.

- In the light of the shared purposes and principles, we are able to tackle the system's most difficult problems with much more confidence and produce more effective results in a much shorter time, while at the same time learning from the mistakes that will inevitably occur.

- Because we are working on a complex adaptive human system of which we are active components, we can never precisely specify the outcome of the reconfiguration process. The Indian philosophy of 'doing work independently of the anticipated outcome' applies here. But without shared purposes and principles we can never know how well we are doing, and what changes we should make to our strategies.

- Without shared purposes and principles there can be no community, no society. With shared purpose, the system comes to life. Shared purpose defines what life means for the system. It provides the inspiration.

Component 3: Soft-systems concepts
Key propositions:

- Soft-systems theory provides the basic concepts and processes for thinking, acting and learning together to understand the configuration of the existing system and to embark purposefully on reconfiguring it.

- By understanding the difference between 'wicked' problems (arising from non-linear systems complexity) and 'tame' problems (arising from the characteristics of linear system), citizens will be able to think, act and learn together successfully.

- Successfully reconfiguring our unjust and unsustainable Global Monetocracy and tackling the wicked problems it has created requires the adoption of a 'purposeful' or systems perspective, rather than mechanistic one.

We have shown two soft-systems concepts, 'shared purposes and principles' and 'participatory change processes', as separate components of the Gaian democracy paradigm. This more general heading brings in the other insights of soft-systems thinking that we introduced in the last section of Chapter 1.

These soft-systems concepts can be used to reconfigure any complex human system from a school or a hospital to a government department, from a neighbourhood to a city to a whole nation. They provide the practical frameworks through which the citizens engaged in participatory change processes keep in close touch with the realities of the system that they and their liberating leaders are trying to improve. They build the knowledge and competencies needed for citizens to work creatively on their 'wicked' problems while observing the shared purposes and principles of the system as a whole.

Through their individual and collective success in reconfiguration processes, citizens and their liberating leaders gain in knowledge, competence and mutual trust. Thus equipped, they are able to tackle ever more complex and difficult 'wicked' problems in their society.

The idea that government could become a learning experience for all concerned, including the leadership, is wholly foreign to command-and-control leaders. The application of these concepts to the political field will transform the way democracy and government works.

Component 4: Paulo Freire's learning principles
Key propositions:

- Dialogue liberates; monologue oppresses.

- The best way to start learning is as part of a dialogue-rich group.

- The richest learning begins with action, is shaped by reflection and leads to further action.

The influence of the Brazilian educationalist Paulo Freire in Latin America and Africa has been enormous. Working originally in the state education system, Freire conceived and developed adult literacy programmes whose purpose was to assist the poorest people to learn to read and write through helping them to respect their own everyday language. Freire insisted that the function of education was to build on the language, experiences and skills of the 'educatees', rather than imposing on them the culture of the 'educators'.

Freire took his literacy programmes out of the classroom and created 'the culture circle'. Here the learners started their studies by using their own way of speaking to build a shared understanding of how their lives came to be as they were, and how they could act to change them. From being a monologue process, education became a process of dialogue in which educatees and educators engaged in mutually respectful learning. Through the culture circles process, people progressed very quickly: in Brazil illiterate adults learned to read and write in 30 hours.[126] Freire pointed out that the astounding results achieved by the culture circles were a consequence of offering literacy as a tool through which groups, rather than individuals, could be empowered. In culture circles, everyone makes good progress, not just a few isolated 'star pupils'.

In 1979 Freire became directly involved in politics and helped to build the Brazilian Workers' Party into the highly effective political movement it is today. His emphasis on the crucial connection between theory and practice can be seen in the way in which the party's mayors introduce radical initiatives like the Participative Budget. From the very poorest to the richest of citizens, they are engaged in a group learning process that will transform their understanding of themselves, each other, their community and the world around them.

A core component of Freirian theory is that learning begins with action, is then shaped by reflection, which gives rise to further action. Learning is thus a continuous process, directed at enhancing the learners' capacity to act in the world and change it. For Freire, whether it is called literacy or learning, this is the principal political task of any society committed to people-power.

In Freire's terms, learning based on group dialogues is liberating for everyone involved in the process. By contrast, teaching based on individual monologues in an imposed language leads to silence and apathy, and is the ultimate form of oppression. In his analysis of the dynamics of power, Freire reserves the term 'oppressed' for those whose own voices are silenced because they are forced to speak with a voice that is not their own: "The oppressed are not only powerless, but reconciled to their powerlessness, perceiving it fatalistically, as a consequence of personal inadequacy or failure. The ultimate product of highly unequal power relationships is a class unable to articulate its own interests or perceive the existence of social conflict." [127]

Component 5: Participatory change processes
Key propositions:

- Participatory change processes enhance the capacity of complex human systems to self-organise, by building ever more precise levels of shared understanding.

- Participatory change processes enable people to thrive in a situation of constant open-ended change, building optimism and trust, commitment, confidence and competence.

- Participatory change processes nurture future liberating leaders.

Command-and-control political leaders often claim that they are willing to consult the people they lead. They do so with a variety of techniques such as polls, surveys or focus groups, by running question and answer sessions at public meetings, receiving delegations or inviting written submissions to specific proposals. Other forms of consultation favoured by more progressive command-and-control leaders include Community Forums, Stakeholder Conferences, Community Planning and joint working parties. The agendas of these processes are usually closely controlled, responsibility for their design and implementation is usually delegated to relatively junior staff, their budgets are niggardly and their impact on core strategies virtually nil. Command-and-control leaders rarely, if ever, take part in them and invariably reserve the right to ignore or veto changes if they are not to their liking.

In these circumstances, it is important to make a clear distinction between what are frequently—and revealingly—called 'participation **exercises**', and the kind of participative change processes that will be a core component of Gaian democracies. 'Participation exercises' rarely produce high levels of shared learning and understanding between the command-and-control leaders, their officials and technical professionals and the people who are lured into offering their contributions.

Liberating political leaders will devote major resources to participative change processes in terms of adequate budgets, high-level expertise and, crucially, their own presence and credibility. Moreover, participative change processes will be the principal means by which core-operating strategies are shaped and monitored by people-power, at every level from the neighbourhood to the society as a whole.

Paulo Freire's concepts of liberating dialogues provide the central design principles of participative change processes. They are the vehicles through which participants can use their own ways of speaking to build a shared understanding of how their world came to be like it is and how to act to change their future. By integrating participative change processes with soft-systems methodologies, the quality of the resultant shared understanding between the participants will be immensely enriched. In practical terms, participative change processes may take just a few hours, a few days or a day a week spread over several months. It could be an open-ended series of processes that go on for years. The number of participants can vary from a small team, to a few dozen to a few hundred, to a few thousand to a few tens of thousands, to—with the help of network and cable TV—hundreds of thousands.[128] Scale is an issue only in terms of the demands it makes on the skills and resources available to the liberating leaders who are responsible for initiating, supporting and sustaining the process.

In all effective participatory processes, the participants do a lot of work in small groups—very like Freire's Culture Circles. The group-work is facilitated to ensure that everybody's contribution is encouraged, heard and respected. A typical process might start with "What are the five most important things we want this process to achieve, for us, for our community, for our children?" The facilitation role is one that requires considerable skill. It may be rotated between the members of the group if they have sufficient confidence, trust and cohesion. Alternatively it may be best for the facilitator to be a skilled 'outsider' whose job it is to serve the group as a whole and not be concerned with making his or her own contribution or getting across a particular point of view.

A typical small-group session lasts about an hour. The general pattern of the process is for the outcomes of all the groups to be openly reviewed at a plenary session in which there are opportunities for further reflection and clarification. The plenary may then break up into another group session and the participants may go back to their original group, or they might randomly re-arrange themselves to form new groups. Different groups might call for specialist advice on some aspect of the system they are reconfiguring. They might call for the production of additional data to clarify a particular issue. If the process is integrated with a soft-systems methodology, the groups might talk about and draw pictures of the systems or sub-systems that need to be changed.

In this way, as the participants think, act and learn together, their shared understanding of the existing situation, and of how to change it for the better, will become ever more precise. Whether there are fifty or five hundred or five thousand or five hundred thousand participants, liberating leaders will devote the time, skills and resources needed to ensure that the participative change processes arrive at good decisions. Such decisions will genuinely reflect the shared information and understanding of the direct participants and their fellow citizens.

At first, many people find such processes confusing and even chaotic. They seem to produce far more energy, information and ideas than can ever be contained and directed effectively. Margaret Wheatley addresses such worries as follows: "I have been in enough experiences with groups of people where we have generated so much information that it's led us to despair and led us to deep confusion. I now know that that's the place to be if you want to really be open to new thoughts, if you want to be totally open to a total reorganizing of your mental constructs or your mind maps, or whatever you want to call them. You can't get there without going through this period of letting go and confusion. For somebody who's been taught to be a good analytical thinker, this is always a very painful moment."[129]

As more and more Gaian citizens actively participate in reconfiguring the systems on which the future of their society depends, instead of resisting change they will positively welcome it. Moreover, the changes arising from participative change processes are usually more comprehensive, radical and sustainable than those which arise from the non-participative change strategies imposed by command-and-control leaders and their enforcers. People-power then ensures that the changes are implemented much more quickly, easily and economically.

Because they encourage dialogue, participative change processes are quite revealing for everyone involved. They provide a multitude of opportunities for citizens to demonstrate their potential as the kind of liberating leaders that Gaian democracies need. In effect their fellow-citizens will identify and encourage them because of the qualities, knowledge and skills they have shown when they were all thinking, acting and learning together.

Component 6: Liberating political leaders
Key propositions:

- Liberating political leaders release the positive potential of people-power.

- Liberating political leaders are committed to their own learning through engaging in the reconfiguration dialogues with their fellow-citizens.

• Liberating political leaders replace a command-and-control culture of monologue with a culture of dialogue.

We gave examples of liberating leaders and how they work in the Summary and Introduction. Good and bad leaders are all around us. Whether they are leading a tennis club, a choir, a hospital, a school or a government department, the differences between good or bad leaders are easy to spot. Ask any group of people to spell out the differences between good leaders and bad leaders, and they will produce a list such as that shown over the page.[130]

There are many good leaders in today's society. The organisations they lead perform consistently well over many years on many criteria, showing outstanding creativity, innovation, efficiency and resilience in harshly competitive environments. These are the kinds of leaders that Gaian democracies will need to develop over the coming years.

One of the most interesting examples is Herb Kelleher, founder and Chief Executive of Southwest Airlines based in Houston, Texas. Since 1970, Southwest Airlines has become the fifth-largest US airline in terms of passengers boarded. It has never had a crash. It has never laid off employees. By 1998, the number of employees had multiplied from the original 195 to 23,000. According to research by Dr Reginald Bruce Management: [131]

"The employees of Southwest enjoy a casual, fun-natured work environment that is celebrated publicly and hard to duplicate. The development of Southwest's company culture emerged when they adopted a philosophy that they wouldn't hide anything, not even any of their problems, from their employees.

"Herb Kelleher's leadership style is the opposite of the many autocratic leaders that have thrived in business for centuries. He does not 'rule' over his employees but rather, rules with his employees. Kelleher believes that leadership is the job of every employee, not just upper level management.

"Kelleher believes that every employee should have the ability to ascertain situations and be able to act on their own decisions.

TABLE 1: Leadership

Good leaders tend to . . .	Bad leaders tend to . . .
be flexible	be inflexible
be competent	value status above skill
be sensitive to people and situations	be aggressive—even physically violent
have clear values and philosophies	have no clear values
admit their mistakes	believe they are infallible
trust and value the people they lead	secretiveness
be decisive—takes decisions well	have no direction, unpredictable
praise more than criticise	play favourites
be versatile	be emotionally blind
be committed to their own development	be lazy
challenge you	make a fool of you in public
listen well and encourage involvement	be remote
be open about their own needs	be condescending
be not afraid to use their power	bully you
be not afraid if you use your power	undermine you
be humble	be humourless
be tough	be ruthless, cowardly, insecure
be able to take criticism	be unable to accept the buck
be stable	be depressed
take risks	be careerists
think clearly	lie to you
delegate and encourage leadership	use calculated abuse
be imaginative	be locked into being 'strong'
protect you	let you down
be approachable, reachable	will not communicate: send you memos
mentor you	talk too much

Employees should be able to lead other employees to make decisions.

"Kelleher's describes Southwest Airlines as 'an upside-down pyramid.' At the bottom, are the upper management personnel and at the top are the front line employees. These front line employees are 'the ones that make things happen'. He considers his front line employees the experts in the organization and top management the support help. The heroes are the front line employees. Kelleher's ability to lead is supported by the leadership offered by all of the employees in the organization.

". . . listening to all employee ideas facilitates leadership. Once employees feel that they have been heard by co-workers, they will be more willing to listen to ideas from others."

Why do the Herb Kellehers of this world resist the pressure to conform to the dominant command-and-control school of leadership? The answer is that their own values and core beliefs are sufficiently powerful to make them search for different ways of running the organisations they lead. Such leaders are in a minority among the vast mass of politicians, bureaucrats and executives whose values and beliefs faithfully reflect those of the elite consensus.

But, although driven by what Peter Drucker called 'an ethical imperative', liberating leaders have a high need for both power and achievement; they are by no means a pushover.[132] The difference lies in their commitment to exercising their power for the benefit of the organisation and fellow-employees, rather than for personal aggrandisement. Most of all, they do not just talk about their values, they constantly and consistently demonstrate them in their behaviours and in the decisions they make. In place of the 'participation exercises' favoured by command-and-control leaders, liberating leaders develop 'a culture of dialogue' in which change comes about through positive people-power. The effect on every member of the organisation of being encouraged to think, act and learn is to constantly improve the efficiency and creativity of the organisation as a whole. For the individuals involved there is an end to the frustration and repression that comes from being undervalued and ignored. As Paulo Freire says, as they learn together through 'problematizing dialogues' (or in our terms, soft-systems methodologies), all the parties begin to liberate themselves from ignorance, fear, injustice, incompetence and prejudice.[133]

Soft-systems processes can be roughly equated with Freire's 'problematizing dialogues', because both seek to "associate the entire population with the task of codifying total reality into symbols which can generate critical consciousness and empower them to alter their relationships with nature and social forces". Thus the men and women who take responsibility for initiating, resourcing, sustaining and legitimating 'a culture of dialogue' can fairly be called 'liberating leaders'.

At present liberating leaders operate almost exclusively in commerce and industry, though there are inspiring exceptions, such as the Workers' Party in Brazil, and doubtless there are some hidden away in the public services of many other countries. But, if Gaian democracies are to replace the Global Monetocracy, liberating leaders will be needed at every level and in every sector of politics, government, public service, finance, industry and commerce.

First of all, liberating leaders will be needed to initiate and grow the local, national and international political movements that will carry the message of Gaian democracies to every corner of the Global Monetocracy. Liberating leaders will be needed to stand as candidates in local and national elections. The political movements they lead will use the basic components of Gaian democracies to configure themselves so that the process of thinking, acting and learning is as natural as breathing to the members and their supporters.

Component 7: Network government [134]
Key propositions:

- Network government will enable Gaian democracies to incorporate Schumacher's principle of 'subsidiarity' at every level from the local to the global.[135]

- Network government enables participatory democracy to be extended beyond the local scale.

- Network government improves societal efficiency, effectiveness and learning by minimising information overload within the different parts of the system.

'Self-organising' and 'self-governing' are different concepts. Within any complex system, it is possible and desirable for sub-systems to be wholly self-organising, but impossible for them to be wholly self-governing. In systems terms, each player in a football team is a self-organising sub-system. But no player is entirely self-governing because there are rules and constraints that have to be obeyed in order to be able to take part in the game.

The Hungarian author and philosopher Arthur Koestler devised the term 'holon' (from the Greek 'holos' meaning 'whole' and the suffix 'on', meaning 'particle' or 'part', as in 'neutron' or 'proton') to describe entities that are simultaneously self-contained wholes as viewed by their subordinated parts, and dependent parts when seen from the inverse direction. In other words, he was describing the basic unit of organisation in biological and social systems.

In network government terms, every player in our football team is a 'holon', i.e. they are each, in the words of John Mathews, "endowed with (their) own processing ability, (their) own autonomy and (their) own 'mind' or 'intelligence'".[136] The team of which they are self-organising holons is called 'a holarchy'. A holarchy is also self-organising by virtue of the nature of the relationships with its holons. Taken to the next level, the team itself is a holon within its own holarchy (or local league). In its turn, the local league is a holon within the holarchy of the national league, and so on up to FIFA (International Federation of Association Football).

Within each holarchy, all the holons have the same basic system-configuration. The basic configuration of Gaian democracies will stem from the seven components we are describing in this chapter. It is a model that offers unlimited scope for diversity, just as the sol-fa system of musical notes has given composers, from Bach to the Beatles and beyond, the framework for unlimited creativity. Even though each Gaian democracy will develop its own local character and dynamic, communications between different levels of holon and holarch democracies will be highly efficient because their basic configurations and self-organising will help to reduce 'noise' and increase 'signal'.

FIGURE 5: Network government

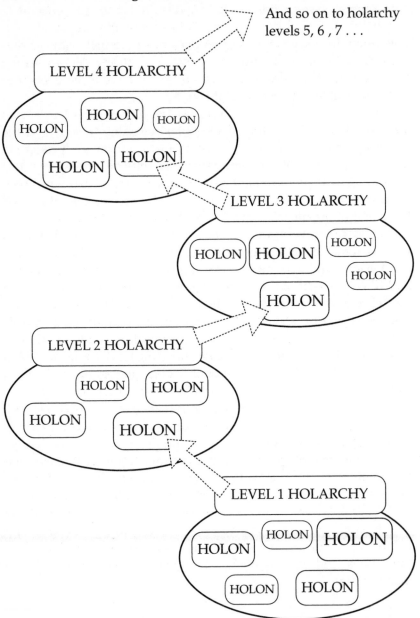

Notes on FIGURE 5 (opposite)
This illustration of a network of holons and holarchies is purely diagrammatic and extremely simplified. It is only intended to show that a holarchy at one level is a holon at the next higher level in the system. The diagram omits any reference to other elements within the system, such as:

- all complex systems are multi-dimensional, not two-dimensional
- movement and change within and between holons and holarchies
- material inputs and outputs
- information channels and flows
- scale and size
- the variations between holons within a holarchy and between holarchies

---

TABLE 2: Applying holon-holarchy terminology to levels of society and government.

Level	Holons	Holarchies
1	Neighbourhoods	Borough
2	Boroughs	City
3	Cities	Region
4	Regions	Nation
5	Nations	Federation
6	Federations	Global Network

Research by Shann Turnbull on the Mondragón cooperatives and Visa International shows that by adopting a system of network government, the tendency to tackle 'wicked' problems through top-down decision-making is minimised. It is also clear that without being configured for network government, complex human systems will increasingly fail to identify, generate and process the information they need to make good decisions. On the other hand, with their limited viewpoints and inadequate capacity to process information, there is no way that top-down decisions-makers can make good decisions. In effect they are overwhelmed by the complexity of the system.

The concept of network government will enable Gaian democracies to make good quality decisions and manage their systems' complexities successfully rather than being overwhelmed by them. In democratic terms, the more self-governing holons there are within the system as a whole, the better it will manage complexity.

Today, political units are tending to become bigger, more centralised and remote. By applying the principles of network government, Gaian democracies' holons will become both smaller and more self-governing, and thus more accessible. What are now big, unmanageable cities could become holarchies, of which the holons are networks of 'city-villages' based on the old ones that the city once swallowed up. At one level this would make for much greater complexity, but through applying their purposes and principles, and the participative change processes and soft-systems methodologies of Gaian Democracy, at every level and between levels, the cities would be much simpler to run.

Within the holarchies we now call nation-states, the holons could be the cities themselves, forming new kinds of democratic-economic systems with a shared purpose and a shared Gaian model of government. Such a political environment should encourage diversity and innovation to flourish, while contributing to the purposes of the system as a whole.

It is impossible to state at this point the principles that Gaian democracies would adopt to regulate relationships within their networks of holarchies and holons. We have already referred to the principle of subsidiarity. Drawing on the experience of Mondragón and Visa, other possibilities include:

- No individuals or groups or sub-systems should be able to dominate democratic deliberations or control decisions.

- All holons and holarchies should incorporate frequent self-critical evaluations of their performance against openly determined multiple criteria.

By disaggregating today's centralised power structures, and placing responsibility for decision-making at the level of the holons and holarchies, Gaian democracies will be shaped by the participative processes through which Gaian citizens have been thinking, acting and learning together. Where there is need for decisions to be made at the level of the whole system, the design of the decision-making process will be undertaken participatively by groups of citizens, professionals and political leaders drawn equitably from its constituent holons and holarchies.

Conclusions

The future is highly unpredictable, and thus every Gaian democracy will be an open-ended learning journey. But there are some things that we can say with confidence about the differences between today's Global Monetocracy and Gaian democracies.

The economy

The most dramatic difference relates to the purpose of the system. The Global Monetocracy is dominated by its purpose of economic growth in order to maintain the debt-money system. As we saw in Chapter 3, it is the controlling imperative for all political and business leaders. As long as the Global Monetocracy remains in being, there is no way round it. And, at the moment, there is no political route out of it.

The very different purposes and principles of Gaian democracies will be developed through the consistent use of people-power. They will reflect the whole range of social, ecological and economic realities with which people and societies have to contend. An early phase in that process will be to take steps to ensure that the Global Monetocracy's growth imperative is switched off or brought to rest. There is no insuperable technical difficulty about this.[137] What is lacking at the moment is not the know-how, but the participative change processes through which citizens can design and implement the transformation.

Ending the creation of debt-money will not necessarily lead to a no-growth economy. The difference will be that, instead of economic growth being shaped by the banks, new forms of economic activity will emerge that reflect their societies' shared purposes and principles. Far more vibrant and diversified economies are likely to develop. Principles concerned with justice and sustainability can be openly discussed and given due weight. The alleviation of all forms of poverty will be a priority both on the grounds of justice and in order to enable all members of the community to participate fully in their economic and political systems.

There is no lack of ideas about the changes that could be made in the money, currency and tax systems in a world freed from the debilitating imperatives of the Global Monetocracy. Several ecologically- and human-friendly systems have been described by James Robertson and Richard Douthwaite in earlier Schumacher Briefings.[138] For example, concurrent money systems, a citizen's income and an international trading currency linked to Gaia's capacity to absorb global warming gases. The existing money system is of course very convenient for the wealthy and successful. But there is no reason why systems which do not rely on debt for the creation of money should not be just as convenient for them, as well as for a far wider class of user—perhaps even more so.

Other proposals generally vetoed by the Global Monetocracy include taxing landowners on site values, community-owned banks and the localisation of economic activity in general. With a global network of thousands of Gaian democracies, these and many other ideas could be explored, adapted, refined and implemented with local variations.

Diversity will be the one feature of the economic systems of the future that can be predicted with confidence. That is how Gaian systems achieve order and flexibility. That will be the inevitable result of addressing 'wicked' problems with a soft-systems approach. Network government will encourage creativity and freedom in the design of all economic systems, in industry and agriculture as well as finance. What we are predicting here is the gradual emergence of a very different world. But it is not one that can be specified, or 'imagineered'. In systems terms, imagineering is inevitably a linear process, and as such cannot take account of the complex adaptive nature of human societies.

There is also a profoundly systemic reason why the components of the Gaian model of democracy do not include a theory of economics. The current neo-liberal theory of economics is derived from a particular set of political purposes and principles that are based on the absolute primacy of private property over all other political and social considerations. They have served the purposes of national—and now global—Monetocracies for over two hundred years. Throughout that time, apart from a few brief intervals, our democratic institutions have been shaped by the imperatives of the debt-based money system. In Gaian democracies, economic instruments and policies will be designed to serve the purposes of justice and sustainability. By changing the purposes of our societies, Gaian democracies will change the basic orientation of our economic instruments and principles. In consequence, new economic theories will be among the many emergent properties of our new system of democracy, not one of its basic components.

Chapter 6

From Principles to Practice

If Gaian democracy is ever to be more than just a pipe dream we now have to tackle the question of how to turn the concept into a practical reality. How—and from where—can the necessary energy, people, skills and resources be mobilised that will generate the matching complexity and variety needed to dismantle and replace the Global Monetocracy with Gaian democracies?

The essentials of successful change

"The world revolution is a revolution not on the streets, but in our minds."— Professor Philip Allott, 1989 Josephine Onoh Memorial Lecture, Hull University

1. Changing the way we think
Put very simply, we have to change the way we think. Fundamental change (as distinct from operational improvements) in any purposeful human system starts to happen when a significant number of people within that system begin to think differently. Surprisingly, there are already significant numbers of people who think in a way that could lead to the co-creation of a global network of Gaian democracies.

We could not have developed this concept without the immense amount of new thinking that is going on in virtually every intellectual discipline in the world today. Thus, although the concept of Gaian democracies as a whole is new, it stems from ways of thinking about the world and societies that are rapidly replacing the ways of thinking which still underpin the Global Monetocracy. The Global Monetocracy's paradigm is directly descended—although much distorted by the passage of time—from the thinking of great luminaries of the past like Plato, Aristotle, Machiavelli, Francis Bacon, René

Descartes and Isaac Newton; also James Madison, Adam Smith, Edmund Burke and Charles Darwin. From those great thinkers comes the vision of all-knowing and powerful elites and the depiction of democracy as mob-rule rather than people-power. In turn, this worldview is closely allied to the drive to conquer and control nature, to separate wholes into their constituent parts and to think of the world as a kind of clockwork machine. Today, with our current knowledge and theoretical insights, we know that basing political and economic ideas on such outdated worldviews is not only highly misleading, it is disastrously wrong.

The Gaian Democracy paradigm arises in response to our current situation, from our vastly greater store of knowledge, and mainly from late 20th century thinking. But it also draws support from a much older tradition of democratic thought that has been suppressed or, at best discounted, over the past three hundred years. As democrats, the ideas of the Athenian democratic philosopher, Protagoras, and his patron, Pericles, are of much more relevance than those of the much better-known, but profoundly anti-democratic, Plato and Aristotle.[139]

In total, the Gaian democracy paradigm reflects our still growing understanding of concepts such as organisational dialogue and learning, soft-systems, cybernetics (the science of communication and control), complexity and chaos theory, symbiosis, inter-dependence and diversity and, of course, Gaia. These concepts are beginning to be understood and applied in almost every field of human endeavour. Thus the shift in thinking that precedes fundamental change is already happening in every sphere outside the closed mind-sets of the Global Monetocracy. What we are doing with the concept of Gaian Democracy is to integrate and focus that new thinking in a new way.

2. The global change-makers

Important though new thinking is, the driving force that kick-starts fundamental change in complex human systems is not coolly rational analysis but warm, deeply felt emotion. Fear, compassion and deep dissatisfaction or anger are powerful drivers for change. Of these, dissatisfaction and anger are perhaps the most powerful. Three different kinds of people are dissatisfied with the Global Monetocracy and all its works. They are:

- **The disaffected insiders.** The people who are trying to make the system work well can become intensely frustrated and even mutinous when the system is not doing what it should be doing, or doing things that they are ashamed to be associated with. In all there are probably hundreds of thousands of such disaffected insiders around the world in parliaments, senates, government departments, city administrations, corporate bureaucracies, universities, schools, hospitals, police forces and NGOs.

- **The angry outsiders.** The agitators and analysts: names like Noam Chomksy, John Pilger, Michael Moore, Susan George, Vandana Shiva, Arianna Huffington, George Monbiot and Waldon Bello come to mind. They can see how badly the system works from the outside, even though they may not be too damaged by it themselves. They gather data, analyse the system's impact, defend its victims and campaign for changes to existing social, environmental and economic policies through books and articles, pressure groups, lobbying, NGOs and mass protests. And for each one we know about or see at anti-globalisation events there are many more like-minded people who do not express their dissatisfaction in public.

- **The system's angry victims.** The people who are really hurt by the system and begin to look for ways to defend themselves, their families and their communities against its depredations. These are usually anonymous workers, peasants, women, children, the poor, the old and the sick.

As we have seen elsewhere, in desperation, a few of the disaffected might turn to one of the many violent forms of opposition. But the vast majority will rightly reject that option as being both morally repugnant and ultimately counter-productive. For them, the possibility of co-creating a global network of Gaian democracies in place of the Global Monetocracy must be worth serious consideration.

Widespread dissatisfaction with the Global Monetocracy

Within the Western 'democracies', the actual numbers of active opponents of the Global Monetocracy are rather small—a few million at most. In Latin America, Africa and many parts of Asia, however, their numbers are very large indeed—tens and possibly hundreds of millions. In Brazil, the landslide victory of the PT's (Brazilian Workers' Party) candidate, Lula da Silva, in the 2002 Presidential elections has deep significance. After the economic collapse of 2002, most Argentinians place the blame for the destruction of their country's economy—and the lives of millions—at the door of the IMF, one of the prime agents of the Global Monetocracy. Wherever one looks in Latin America—Bolivia, Venezuela, Ecuador—the examples multiply. Similar accounts of mass anger can be found in the Philippines, Japan and Indonesia. Almost every country in Africa is an economic basket case, with rising levels of poverty, misery and civil unrest as the norm. As for the former Soviet Union, tens of millions of citizens are simmering with futile rage at the closeness with which ex-communists and organised crime have collaborated to create corrupt and reactionary 'kleptocracies', under the benign guidance of the World Bank, the IMF and Western economic advisers.

Even within the Western 'democracies', although the symptoms are more muted, the rising levels of disaffection are plain to see. Only 39% of US citizens voted in the 2002 mid-term elections, only 62 % of British voters turned out at the 2001 General Election, and an average of less than 25% voted in the British mayoral elections, which were designed to reinvigorate local democracies.

All around the planet, the real and rising levels of disaffection with the Global Monetocracy presents its opponents with a historic opportunity. So far the conventional forms of opposition have not made the slightest impact. Many brave defensive battles have been fought and some have been won—for the time being. But, where there should be a strategy for change there is a vacuum. That is why we believe that the vision of a global network of Gaian democracies could enable global disaffection to be focused on effective political action for change at local, national and global levels.

Are we capable of co-creating a global network of Gaian democracies?

We have inherited the genes of our hunter-gatherer ancestors. They are unlikely to have worried about global issues, or to have made long-term plans. There was nothing in their environment that would have favoured such behaviours. In his Environment Foundation lecture in November 2001, Professor Richard Dawkins warned against relying on our genes to somehow get us through in the long-term: "Short-term genetic benefit is all that matters in a Darwinian world. Superficially, the values that will have been built into us will have been short-term values, not long-term ones. . . . If it were left to Darwinism alone there would be no hope. Short term greed is bound to win."

We can watch what happens to yeast in a sugar pot; we have seen what rabbits do in Australia, and what deer did in St Matthew's Island. A species in invasion mode will extend itself into every available ecological niche until exhaustion and collapse. Humans are no different. Ten thousand years ago the total world population of human beings is thought to have been somewhere between a few hundred thousand and a few million.[140] Since then our numbers have rocketed to six billion and we have spread out to overrun the whole planet. In the meantime, many human civilisations have collapsed because they undermined their local environment. And, as we saw in Chapter 2, invasion mode is precisely the mode the entire human family is in today. We have no gene for long-term species survival, and, as Professor Dawkins says: "What it means is that we must work all the harder for the long-term future, in spite of getting no help from nature, precisely because nature is not on our side . . ."

All hunter-gatherers operate in highly cooperative small groups, so it seems that we are probably genetically designed to cooperate on this scale. But we do not have a gene for large-scale cooperation. We are not genetically designed to cooperate in societies with many thousands of members, never mind millions or billions. So we have to make a positive effort to cooperate on this scale, now that the world situation calls for it—hence the importance of concepts such as network government to make such cooperation possible on any scale from the local to the global.

Making rational and realistic choices

Human beings are endowed with contradictory genetic predispositions. We are capable of being both greedy and generous, violent and tender, devious and direct, careless and cautious, competitive and cooperative, thoughtful and impulsive. Of crucial significance, though overlooked—indeed denied—by the Global Monetocracy, is the fact that healthy human beings have a powerful genetic predisposition to want to give—and go on giving—the best of ourselves to each other and to the world around us. Thus we are far from being at the mercy of our short-term greed. Instead, given half a chance, it is our capacity to give and receive love that could generate the energy and creativity needed for success.

The particular mix of genetic predispositions that drives our behaviour depends on a variety of factors: the specific situation, the cultural context, our upbringing, training and conditioning, our physical and psychological health, the benefits or penalties that might ensue, to name but a few. What certainly helps to improve the choices we make is the chance to gather information and explore different options with a group of people we can trust. That is when our big brains begin to work cooperatively, and where we can consciously override some of our genetic predispositions, and nurture others.

What is true of individuals is also true for communities. Instead of genetic predispositions, communities have cultural dispositions based on the norms and values of their most influential groups. Communities with many conflicting groups will have conflicting cultural dispositions. These will arise from conflicting values and conflicting information. Each will powerfully influence the decisions that communities and groups within society will take, and the way that they will take them. And, just as in certain circumstances individuals can decide which of their genetic predispositions should take precedence, so too communities and groups can—in certain circumstances—choose to give greater weight to certain values and norms, and thus change their collective behaviours.

The vast sums spent by states and corporations on advertising and public relations in order to 'manufacture consent' for their policies and values do have some effect. In his TV series, *The Century of the Self,* Adam Curtis highlighted the urge for instant individual gratification over the long-term good of the community and traced it to the efforts of the public relations and advertising industries.[141] Even so, millions of people are acutely aware that greed and selfishness is anti-social. The net effect of the huge sums spent on manufacturing consent is that the majority of citizens now assume that all politicians and political parties are unworthy of trust. Better not to vote for any of them than to collude in a fatally compromised and dysfunctional system.

As long as the Global Monetocracy goes unchallenged as a total system, the citizens who disengage themselves from politics at any level are taking rational and realistic decisions. New political parties, offering their fellow-citizens a vision of Gaian Democracy will encourage their active participation in co-creating a global network of just and sustainable societies. The combination of a new vision and a new kind of democracy is what is needed to revive popular commitment to active citizenship.

Can the Gaian Democracy model work in the real world?

As we described in the Introduction to this Briefing, even within the command-and-control culture of the Global Monetocracy, some liberating leaders have been able to bring some of the components of the Gaian Democracy model together in either a governmental or a business setting.

The strictly economic and operational successes of these initiatives are very impressive in themselves. But each example also shows that there are immeasurable qualitative benefits for the people involved. It is those factors that enable us to argue that the concept of active citizenship, which lies at the heart of Gaian Democracy, is not dead and buried—it is merely anaesthetised and waiting to be revived.

The benefits of Gaian citizens exercising their democratic responsibilities will be immense, both individually and collectively. In *We, the People*, Perry Walker of the New Economics Foundation cites research studies from Switzerland showing that active participation in political decision-making dramatically increases the number of people who say that they are very happy.[142] American studies cited by him show that participants become more aware of public issues, and become more actively involved in civic activities. And almost all who have taken part in genuine participative processes said they would like to repeat the experience. He reports that after even a relatively low-level participative experience, the number who said that they had opinions about politics that were worth listening to rose from 40% to 68%. Participants in Citizen Juries, said that they "were more confident", "felt a better person", "wanted to contribute more", and had been "changed for life".

Apart from the human benefits, there are substantial practical benefits derived from the much better quality decisions that arise from the much more comprehensive range of information and ideas that active citizens generate and integrate. Such benefits are unavailable to the command-and-control leaders of the Global Monetocracy. The current political paradigm is specifically designed to deny citizens the chance to give expression to even a fraction of the competence, the knowledge and the ideas they possess. By contrast, the Gaian Democracy paradigm is designed to liberate the competence, knowledge and ideas of active citizens, and nourish their capacities for liberating leadership.

The operational success of the examples we have given can be attributed to their development of structures and processes whose complexity matches the complex environments that they have to contend with. To repeat Shann Turnbull's words: "The challenge for developing *a new way to govern* is to determine the simple basic design rules to create organisations [or as we would say, Gaian democracies] that manage complexity along the same principles evolved in nature. The reason for following the rules of nature to construct ecological organisations is that these rules have proved to be the most efficient and robust way to create and manage complexity."[143]

How competent will Gaian democracies be?

The Mondragón Cooperatives, Athenian democracy, modern Brazil, the Semco corporation and Visa International show some the components of Gaian democracies at work in the real world. In every case they illustrate the need for liberating leadership, whether in the business world, as with Dee Hock, Ricardo Semler or José Maria

Arrizmendi-Arrieta, or in government, as shown by Kleisthenes and the Brazilian Workers' Party. They show that dialogue-based people-power is immensely rewarding for all of the people concerned and for the system as a whole. They suggest the wide diversity of the situations in which the Gaian Democracy model could be applied. And they all show that the kinds of changes involved in creating Gaian democracies can be peacefully initiated and sustained by liberating leaders who are prepared to think and work outside the dominant command-and-control paradigm.

Over the past two hundred years, businesses, and to a lesser extent the public services, have unwittingly acted as a vast laboratory for developing our understanding of how purposeful human systems work. As our examples show, the concepts and values underpinning Gaian Democracy have been tested and refined by hard-pressed managers and politicians in response to the needs of their specific circumstances. We have cited only a few, but there are many more and some of them are on *www.wwdemocracy.org*.

The literature of people-powered systems change is enormous. What has been missing so far is a comprehensive theory of people-powered change for complex political systems, an omission we have tried to remedy in Chapter 5.

In the business field, Professor W. Edwards Deming provided the nearest approach to a comprehensive theory of organisational change with the work he did with Bell Telephones in the 1930s, the US Bureau of Census and Department of Defense in the 1940s, and most of all, the shattered remnants of Japanese industry from 1950 onwards.[144] Deming's approach was summed up in a list of fourteen points, including:

- Adopt the new philosophy

- Constantly improve the system

- Institute leadership and stop managing

- Eliminate numerical quotas

- Break down barriers

- Eliminate slogans and targets

- Remove barriers to workers' pride

- Education and the quantum leap

- Involve everyone in the transformation

Like most systems and organisational thinkers, Deming largely avoided discussing the wider social and political implications of his work. However, Japanese industry credits him with showing them how to raise the post-war remnants of their industry from an uncompetitive, inefficient and imitative also-ran to the world leader in quality, productivity and innovation that it is today. The implications of what Deming taught the Japanese and the way they applied his ideas are still not generally understood by the business, political and academic elites of the Global Monetocracy. Although some attempts have been made to copy the operational techniques that arise from his thinking—notably quality circles and so-called 'lean' manufacturing—the importance of embracing the totality of his ideas has been ignored. In the light of Chapter 3, this is not surprising. Deming's points embody a fundamental change in leadership values, and an adoption of a vast range of systems concepts and methodologies at every level in the organisation.

On the other hand, even though they were not aware of Deming's ideas, many business and political leaders have independently applied profoundly systemic and intensely human ways of thinking to thousands of business and public service organisations. The practical improvements they produce in the pursuit of their purposes make it reasonable to predict that Gaian democracies will be similarly effective in pursuit of their aims.

The examples we gave are very encouraging. Porto Alegre is constantly cited as being one of the best-run cities in the world. Semco not only survived but prospered mightily while the IMF and the World Bank guided the rest of the Brazilian manufacturing sector into crisis after crisis. The Mondragón cooperatives consistently produced far better profits and returns on capital than conventional capitalist companies. Visa International is a trillion-dollar business conducting billions of monetary exchanges between millions of clients in every country in the world, and absorbs the demands put upon it without faltering.

In every case their achievements stem from their capacity to handle complexity competently and creatively rather than being overwhelmed by it. The elite consensus and operational theories on which the Global Monetocracy and its national branch offices are based make it impossible for them to transform themselves to handle competently the exploding complexity we are now facing from our internal and external environments.

Thus, the bottom line for the human family is that, without the collective competence that Gaian democracies generate, the 'wicked' problems we face will get worse and worse. The elites of the Global Monetocracy insist that 'the bewildered herd' is incapable of thinking, acting and learning together to overcome the problems we face. **Nothing could be further from the truth**. The competencies that Gaian democracies will generate will open up the possibilities for our societies to deal effectively with the most intractable of our current dilemmas. The examples we have given show that almost anything is possible through people of all ages and backgrounds thinking, acting and learning together. By doing this we believe that the dream of a just and sustainable future for humanity can become a practical reality.

The Gaian Democracy model is open to a great deal of further co-development and co-learning from many disciplines. We hope you will join the forum for dialogue and learning we have set up at *www.wwdemocracy.org*. Alternatively, if you would like to start working on the Gaian democracies political project, please contact us via *www.gaiandemocracies.net*, or call from within the UK on 0845 458 3919.

References

Introduction and Summary: **Redefining Globalisation and People-Power**

1. For example, see the Hadley Centre for Climate Prediction and Research at http://www.met-office.gov.uk/research/hadleycentre/; and the International Geosphere-Biosphere Program at http://www.igbp.kva.se/cgi-bin/php/frameset.php

2. For an excellent discussion of the difference between social change and social defence see George Lakey, 'Human Shields in Palestine and Pushing Our Thinking About People Power: Part Two' at www.zmag.org/sustainers/content/2002-06/01lakey.cfm

3. David Held (ed.), *A Globalizing World?: Culture, Economics, Politics (Understanding Social Change)*, Routledge, London, 2000.

4. Shann Turnbull, *A New Way to Govern*, a paper presented to the Organisations and Institutions Network, 14th Annual Meeting on Socio-Economics, University of Minnesota, Minnesota, USA, June 27-30, 2002.

5. For example, see Shann Turnbull, 'Curing The Cancer In Capitalism With Employee Ownership' at *http://cog.kent.edu/lib/TurnbullCuringCancerForConference.htm*; The National Center for Employee Ownership at *www.nceo.org*; and Employee Ownership Options at *www.employee-ownership.org.uk*.

6. Ricardo Semler, *Maverick!*, Century, London, 1993.

7. John Dunn in the preface to John Dunn (ed.), *Democracy; The Unfinished Journey 508 BC to AD 1993*, OUP, Oxford, 1992.

8. This is the best known of a number of innovations in participatory democracy being conducted by the PT in Brazil, the Frente Amplio (Broad Front) in Uruguay, and elsewhere in South America. See the MOST Clearing House for further examples at *www.unesco.org/most/bphome.htm*.

Chapter 1: **A New Language of Change**

9. See the 'Systems thinking' section of *www.wwdemocracy.org* for examples.

10. Fritjof Capra is one of the leading advocates and exponents of the application of systems thinking to the dilemmas that the human family is facing. See his latest book, *The Hidden Connections*, HarperCollins, London, 2002.

11. 'The New Science of Leadership: An Interview with Margaret Wheatley' by Scott London, from the radio series *Insight & Outlook* at *www.scottlondon.com/insight/scripts/wheatley.html* See also Samir Rihani, *Complex Systems Theory and Development Practice: Understanding Non-linear Realities*, Zed Books, London, 2002.

12. See Stafford Beer, *The Heart of the Enterprise*, J. Wiley & Sons, London, 1979.

13. Peter Senge, *The Fifth Discipline: the Art and Practice of the Learning Organisation*, Doubleday/Currency, New York, 1990. p.79.

14. Ibid.

15. Fritjof Capra, *The Web of Life*, HarperCollins, London, 1996.

16. Peter Checkland, *Systems Thinking, Systems Practice*, John Wiley & Sons Ltd, Chichester, 1981.

17. E. Jeffrey Conklin & William Weil in 'Wicked Problems: Naming The Pain in Organisations', *3M Meeting News*, (based on the work of Professor Horst Rittel). See *www.touchstone.com/tr/wp/wicked.html*

18. Muriel Rukeyser, *Willard Gibbs: American Genius*, Doubleday, NY, 1942, p445.

19. See the website of the Chaordic Commons at *www.chaordic.org/what_des.html*

20. Jake Chapman, *System Failure: Why governments must learn to think differently*, Demos, London, 2002. p.63.

21. See John McMurtry, *Unequal Freedoms: The Global Market as an Ethical System*, Kumarian Press, Bloomfield, 1998.

22. See Hartmut Bossel, *Earth At The Crossroads: Paths to a Sustainable Future*, Cambridge University Press, Cambridge, 1998.

Chapter 2: Humanity in a Vicious Spiral

23. See Herbert Girardet, *Earthrise: How Can We Heal Our Injured Planet?*, Paladin Books, London, 1992.

24. See *Global Environmental Outlook-3 (Geo-3)* report of the United Nations Environment Group, Earthscan, London, 2002.

25. See Luca Tacconi, *Biodiversity and Ecological Economics*, Earthscan, London, 2001.

26. Steve Connor, 'How one creature drives so many species to extinction', *The Independent*, 21 May 2002.

27. *Living Planet Report*, WWF, July 2002. See *www.panda.org/news_facts/publications/general/livingplanet/lpr02.cfm*.

28. Reported by BBC News Online environment correspondent Alex Kirby in 'Nature Pays Biggest Dividends', 8 Aug 2002. See *http://news.bbc.co.uk/2/hi/science/nature/2179291.stm*

29. E.O. Wilson (ed.), *Biodiversity*, National Academy of Sciences/Smithsonian Institution, Washington, 1988.

30. See Pooran Desai & Sue Riddlestone, *Bioregional Solutions*, Schumacher Briefing No 8, p.27.

31. E.F Schumacher, *Small is Beautiful: A Study Of Economics As If People Mattered*, Blond & Briggs Ltd, London, 1973.

32. *Living Planet Report*, op cit.

33. See Richard Douthwaite, *Short Circuit*, Green Books, Totnes, 1996; Helena Norberg-Hodge, Todd Merrifield & Steven Gorelick, *Bringing the Food Economy Home*, Kumarian Press, Bloomfield, 2002; and Vandana Shiva, *Stolen Harvest: The Hijacking of the Global Food Supply*, Southend Press, Cambridge MA, 1999.

34. Herbert Girardet, 'Global Village or Global Pillage', *Resurgence*, Jan/Feb 2003, p.6.

35. See interview with Colin Campbell at *www.fromthewilderness.com/free/ww3/102302_campbell.html*. See also *www.hubbertpeak.com*

36. See Tony Boys, *Causes and Lessons of the "North Korean Food Crisis"*. Paper for the Ibaraki Christian University Junior College, Japan, at *www9.ocn.ne.jp/~aslan*.

37. Rachel Carson, *Silent Spring*, Hamish Hamilton, London, 1963.

38. Theo Colborn, Dianne Dumanoski & John Peterson Myers, *Our Stolen Future*, Plume, New York, 1996, p.242.

39. Theo Colborn et al, op cit., p.241.

40. Ibid., p.243.

41. Mae Wan Ho, *Genetic Engineering: Dream or Nightmare?*, Continuum, NY, 1998, p.10.

42. See Arjun Makhijani, *Ecology and Genetics: An Essay on the Nature of Life and the Problem of Genetic Engineering*, Institute for Energy and Environmental Research, Apex Press, NY, 2001.

43. Theo Colborn et al, op cit., p.241.

44. See George Monbiot, 'What do we really want?', *The Guardian*, 27 Aug 2002.

45. See Jon E. Hilsenrath, 'Happiness has its price', *The Wall Street Journal*, 4 Jan 2002.

46. See John Adams, *The Social Implications of Hypermobility*, Report for OECD Project on Environmentally Sustainable Transport, ENV/EPOC/PPC/T(99)3/FINAL, Paris, 1999.

47. Quoted by Ian Christie in Robert Hutchison (ed.), *Ahead of Time—Birthday Letters to Mayer Hillman*, Policy Studies Institute, London, 2001, p.25.

48. See Martin Khor, 'Global Economy and the Third World' in Edward Goldsmith & Jerry Mander (eds.), *The Case Against the Global Economy and For a Turn to the Local*, Earthscan, London, 2001, p.146.

49. Oswaldo de Rivero, *The Myth of Development*, Zed Books, 2001, NY, p.125.

50. Wayne Ellwood, *The No-Nonsense Guide to Globalisation*, Verso, London, 2002, p.97.

51. Thomas Frank, *One Market Under God: Extreme Capitalism, Market Populism, and the End of Economic Democracy*, Doubleday, NY, 2000—quoted by Russell Mockhiber and Robert Weissman in *Corporate Crime Reporter*, 2 December 2000.

52. See for example Center on Budget and Policy Priorities reports at www.cbpp.org/

53. *Forbes* 16th annual ranking of billionaires, 2002. See www.forbes.com/2002/02/28/billionaires.html

54. See 'Engineering Solutions to Malnutrition', *The Seedling*, March 2000 (www.grain.org/publications/mar002-en.cfm). Reproduced in *The Irish Seed Saver*, Summer 2000.

55. Mark Weisbrot, Dean Baker, Egor Kraev & Judy Chen, *The Scorecard on Globalization 1980-2000: Twenty Years of Diminished Progress*, Center for Economic and Policy Research, Washington, 2001.

56. UK government statistics discussed by John Carvel in '70% of children in care achieve no exam passes', *The Guardian*, 13 Oct 2000.

57. Samir Rihani, *Complex Systems Theory and Development Practice: Understanding Non-linear Realities*, Zed Books, London, 2002, p.211.

58. Ibid., p.251.

59. Research by Professor James Alcock, Penn State-Abington University, reported by Cat Lazaroff, 'Amazon rainforest could be unsustainable within a decade', *Environment News Service*, 26 Jun 2001.

60. See Andy Solomon, 'Antarctic Ice Melt May Come in Next Generation', Yahoo News, at http://www.physics.ohio-state.edu/~kagan/phy367/P367_articles/GreenHouseEffect/warming.html

61. David Keys, 'Methane threatens to repeat Ice Age meltdown', *The Independent*, 16 Jun 2001.

62. Interview with Geoff Jenkins, Head of the Hadley Centre for Climate Prediction and Research, Reuter News Service, UK, 14 May 2002. See www.global-warming.net/fasterthanexpected.htm

63. See 'Grassland Responses to Global Environmental Changes Suppressed by Elevated CO2', *Science*, 6 Dec 2002.

64. See Claude T. Allégre & Stephen H. Schneider, 'The Evolution Of The Earth', *Scientific American*, No 271, Oct 1994, p.44-51.

65. Theo Colborn et al, op cit., p.239.

Chapter 3: **The Global Monetocracy**

66. See James Robertson, *Transforming Economic Life*, Schumacher Briefing No. 1; and Richard Douthwaite, *The Ecology of Money*, Schumacher Briefing No. 4. See also Joseph Huber & James Robertson, *Creating New Money: A Monetary Reform for the Information Age*, New Economics Foundation, London, 2000; and Michael Rowbotham, *The Grip of Death*, J. Carpenter Publishing, Oxford, 1998.

67. James Robertson, *The Alternative Mansion House Speech*, New Economics Foundation, London, 2000, p.6. See http://attac.org.uk/attac/html/view-document.vm?documentID=84

68. John McMurtry, *Value Wars: The Global Market Versus the Life Economy*, Pluto Press, London, 2002, p.129.

69. See Joseph Huber & James Robertson, op cit.

70. See the Index of Sustainable Economic Welfare (ISEW) website at www.foe.co.uk/campaigns/sustainable_development/progress/

71. See Samir Rihani, op cit.

72. See Michael Rowbotham, *Goodbye America! Globalisation, Debt and the Dollar Empire*, J. Carpenter Publishing, Oxford, 2000.

73. See Joseph Stiglitz reviewing George Soros, *On Globalisation*, PublicAffairs Ltd, NY, 2002, in *The New York Review of Books*, 23 May 2002. Debt payments are not the only reason for the flow: people in poor countries invest in rich countries to get a better return on their money.

74. For example, see Hugo Salinas Price, 'What really killed Argentina?' at www.plata.com.mx/plata/comHSP29a.htm

75. *New Internationalist*, November 2002, p.19.

76. Bob Sutcliffe, *100 Ways of Seeing an Unequal World*, Zed Books, NY, 2001, p.91.

77. George Soros, *On Globalisation*, PublicAffairs Ltd, NY, 2002. Quoted in review by Joseph Stiglitz in *The New York Review of Books*, 23 May 2002.

78. Joseph Stiglitz reviewing George Soros, ibid.

79. John Maynard Keynes, *The General Theory of Employment, Interest and Money*, 1936, p.1.

80. Susan George, 'Winning the War of Ideas', *Dissent*, Summer 1997.

81. Ibid.

82. For example, Guy Routh in *The Origins of Economic Ideas*, Macmillan Press, London, 1975; the Australian economist Steve Keen in *Debunking Economics: The Naked Emperor of Social Sciences*, Pluto Press, Sydney, 2001; and The Richard T. Ely Lectures by Professor Kenneth J. Boulding 1965, Prof Joan Robinson 1971, J.K. Galbraith 1972.

83. John McMurtry, 'What economics hides: the paradigm revolution' article posted 16 Jun 2001 on the MAI-NOT network. See http://mai.flora.org/forum/27059.

84. John Gray, *False Dawn: The Delusions of Global Capitalism*, Granta, London, 1998. p.17.

85. See Richard Swift, *The No-Nonsense Guide to Democracy*, Verso, London, 2002.

86. In the course of his 'keynote' speech at a recent Charter 88 conference on 'The Future of Democracy'. See www.privy-council.org.uk/output/page291.asp

87. Attributed to Tony Blair by Andrew Rawnsley in *Servants of the People*, Penguin, London, 2001, p 195; quoted by Robin Ramsay in *The Rise of New Labour*, Pocket Essentials, Harpenden, 2002. The statement is true whether or not Blair actually said this. For our purposes, it confirms the inability of ordinary people to influence policy through political parties.

88. See David Held, *Democracy and the Global Order*, Polity Press, Cambridge, 1995; and David Held, Anthony McGrew, David Goldblatt & Jonathon Perraton, *Global Transformations: Politics, Economics and Culture*, Polity Press, Cambridge, 1999.

89. See George Monbiot, *Captive State*, Macmillan, London, 2000; John R. Macarthur, *Selling Free Trade: NAFTA, Washington and the Subversion of American Democracy*, Hill & Wang, NY, 2000; Vandana Shiva, *Biopiracy: The Plunder of Nature and Knowledge*, South End Press, Cambridge MA, 1997; and Vandana Shiva, *Protect or Plunder*, Zed Books, London, 2001.

90. See John Gray, op cit.

91. Philip Allott, *The Health of Nations: Society and Law Beyond the State*, C.U.P., Cambridge, 2002, p.409.

92. Especially the World Business Council for Sustainable Development.

93. See www.corporateeurope.org or contact ceo@corporateeurope.org

94. Noam Chomsky, 'Media Control', *Alternative Press Review*, Fall 1993 (reprinted from *Open Magazine*).

95. Walter Lippman, *Public Opinion*, 1922.

96. Noam Chomsky, *Media Control: The Spectacular Achievements of Propaganda (The Open Media Pamphlet Series, No. 1)*, Seven Stories Press, NY, 1997.

97. As with the protests against the Poll Tax in the UK, the Reclaim the Streets and Anti-WTO Campaigns.

98. As demonstrated in Adam Curtis's TV series, *The Century of the Self*, shown on BBC 2 in the Spring of 2002.

99. Edward Herman & Noam Chomsky, *Manufacturing Consent: the Political Economy of the Mass Media*, Pantheon Books, NY, 1988, p.303.

100. Numerous independent agencies monitor government, corporate and corporate media attempts to manufacture consent for actions and policies that are scandalous or illegal. In particular, see *www.prwatch.org* and *www.medialens.org*.

101. Dean Anderson & Linda Ackerman, 'How Command-and-control as a Change Leadership Style Causes Transformational Change Efforts to Fail', *Results From Change*, Issue 7, 1 Jun 2002. See *www.beingfirst.com/resultsfromchange/200206.html*.

102. CS Holling* & Gary Meffe, *Command-and-control and the Pathology of Natural Resource Management*, *Department of Zoology, University of Florida & University of Georgia's Savannah River Ecology Laboratory, SREL reprint 2078.

103. See Jake Chapman, op cit.

104. See Helmut Bossel, op cit.; John Gray, op cit.; Christopher Lasch, *The Revolt of the Elites*, Norton & Co, NY, 1995; John McMurtry, *Unequal Freedoms*, op cit.; Robert H. Nelson, *Economics as Religion: From Samuelson to Chicago and Beyond*, Penn State UP, PA, 2001; and John Ralston-Saul, *Voltaire's Bastards: The Dictatorship of Reason in the West*, Penguin, Toronto, 1992.

105. See *www.opensecrets.org/bush/cabinet.asp*.

106. George Monbiot, 'As we know from bombing Serbia: refineries are the key', *The Guardian*, 14 Sep 2000.

107. George Monbiot, 'Rout of the small farm', *The Guardian*, 7 Aug 2001.

108. Mark Townsend, 'Top bosses 'hijacking' eco-summit', *The Observer*, 21 Mar 2002.

109. George Monbiot, 'Wreckers unite', The Guardian 19th Feb 2002.

110. Bruce Johnston, 'Berlusconi, Blair and the Italian connection', *The Daily Telegraph*, 16 Feb 2002.

111. See Norman Myers & Jennifer Kent, *Perverse Subsidies: How Misused Tax Dollars Harm the Environment and the Economy*, Island Press, Washington DC, 2001.

112. George Monbiot, 'Why Blair is an appeaser', *The Guardian*, 5 Nov 2002.

113. Mae Wan Ho, op cit., p 10.

114. PBS interview with Kevin Phillips on *Now with Bill Moyers*. See *www.pbs.org/now/transcript/transcript_phillips.html*.

115. William E. Rees, 'Squeezing the Poor', *Toronto Star*, 22 Apr 2002.

Chapter 4: A Political Vacuum

116. See Jeremy Leggett, *The Carbon War: Global Warming and the End of the Oil Era*, Routledge, London, 2001.

117. The aggregate cut of 5.2% against 1990 levels by 2008-12 has been reduced to 1.5%. See 'Kyoto protocol finally gets the green light', *ENDS Environmental Daily*, 12 Nov 2001.

118. Joseph Stiglitz, *Globalization and its Discontents*, Penguin, London, 2002.

119. 'CEOs: Why They're So Unloved', editorial in *Business Week*, 22 Apr 2002.

120. See *www.citizen.org/trade/issues/mai/articles.cfm?ID=7615*.

121. Speech to the founding meeting of the UK branch of ATTAC, attended by the authors.

122. 'What is global civil society?' CIVNET Journal Jan/Feb 1999 Vol 3 No 1.

Chapter 5: Gaian Democracies

123. See Eugene Odum, 'Environmental Ethics and the Attitude Revolution' in William Blackstone (ed.). *Philiosophy and Environmental Crisis*, University of Georgia Press, Athens GA, 1974.

124. James Lovelock, 'Elements', *Living Lightly*, Issue 19, Spring 2002, p 17.

125. See Dee Hock, Birth of the Chaordic Age, Berrett-Koehler Publishers, San Francisco, 1999.

126. See Paulo Freire, *Cultural Action for Freedom (Harvard Educational Review Monograph Series No 1)*, Harvard Education Publishing Group, Cambridge MA, 1970.

127. Ibid.

128. For examples, see *www.wwdemocracy.org*.

129. Interview with Margaret Wheatley, op cit.

130. Responses to initial discussions at leadership workshops conducted by Roy Madron.

131. See Eun Kim, Fred Liggin, Genita McKinney, Keith Norris & Sonya Owens for Dr. Reginald Bruce Management, 'Southwest Airlines 25 Years of LUV'. See *http://cbpa.louisville.edu/bruce/cases/swa2/swa2.htm*.

132. See Peter Drucker, *The Practice of Management*, Heinemann, London, 1955.

133. See Paulo Freire, *Pedagogy of the Oppressed*, Continuum, NY, 1970.

134. Much of the material used in this section is taken from Shann Turnbull's paper to the first Global Brain Workshop, Brussels, July 2001: 'Design Criteria For A Global Brain (revised Sep 2001)'. See *http://pespmc1.vub.ac.be/Conf/GB-0.html*.

135. See E.F. Schumacher, op cit.

136. John Mathews, 'Holonic Organisational Architecture', *Human Systems Management*, Vol. 15, No. 1, 1996.

137. See Joseph Huber & James Robertson, op cit.

138. James Robertson, *Transforming Economic Life,* Schumacher Briefing No. 1; Richard Douthwaite, *The Ecology of Money*, Schumacher Briefing No. 4; Aubrey Meyer, *Contraction and Convergence*, Schumacher Briefing No. 5. See also Alan Twelvetrees (ed.), *Community Economic Development: Rhetoric or Reality?*, Community Development Foundation, London, 1998.

Chapter 6: **From Principles to Practice**

139. See John Dunn, op cit.

140. See US Census Bureau summary of historical estimates of world population at *http://www.census.gov/ipc/www/worldhis.html*.

141. Shown on BBC 2, March 2002.

142. Perry Walker, *We the People*, New Economics Foundation Notebook, London, 2002. See also Bruno Frey & Alois Stutzer, *Happiness and Economics*, Princeton University Press, Princeton, 2002.

143. Shann Turnbull, *A New Way to Govern*, op cit.

144. W. Edwards Deming, *Out of the Crisis*, MIT Center for Advanced Engineering Study, Cambridge, MA, 1986.

Bibliography

Systems & Complexity

Philip Allott, *The Health of Nations: Society and Law Beyond the State*, C.U.P., Cambridge, 2002.

Stafford Beer, *The Heart of the Enterprise*, J. Wiley & Sons, London, 1979.

Hartmut Bossel, *Earth At The Crossroads: Paths To A Sustainable Future*, Cambridge University Press, Cambridge, 1998.

Fritjof Capra, *The Hidden Connections*, HarperCollins, London, 2002.

Fritjof Capra, *The Web of Life*, HarperCollins, London, 1996.

Jake Chapman, *System Failure: Why governments must learn to think differently*, Demos, London, 2002.

Peter Checkland, *Systems Thinking, Systems Practice*, John Wiley & Sons Ltd, Chichester, 1981.

Peter Checkland, *Soft Systems Methodology in Action*, John Wiley & Sons Ltd, Chichester, 1999.

Leopold Kohr, *The Breakdown of Nations*, Green Books, Totnes, 2001.

Samir Rihani, *Complex Systems Theory and Development Practice: Understanding Non-linear Realities*, Zed Books, London, 2002.

Peter Senge, *The Fifth Discipline: the Art and Practice of the Learning Organisation*, Doubleday/Currency, New York, 1990.

Economics & Finance

Richard Douthwaite, *The Ecology of Money*, Schumacher Briefing No. 4.

Richard Douthwaite, *Short Circuit*, Green Books, Totnes, 1996.

Thomas Frank, *One Market Under God: Extreme Capitalism, Market Populism, and the End of Economic Democracy*, Doubleday, NY, 2000.

Bruno Frey & Alois Stutzer, *Happiness and Economics*, Princeton University Press, Princeton, 2002.

Edward Goldsmith & Jerry Mander (eds.), *The Case Against the Global Economy and for a Turn to the Local*, Earthscan, London, 2001.

John Gray, *False Dawn: The Delusions of Global Capitalism*, Granta, London, 1998.

Joseph Huber & James Robertson, *Creating New Money: A Monetary Reform for the Information Age*, New Economics Foundation, London, 2000.

Steve Keen, *Debunking Economics: The Naked Emperor of Social Sciences*, Pluto Press, Sydney, 2001.

John Maynard Keynes, *The General Theory of Employment, Interest and Money*, Harcourt, Brace & Company, 1936.

Leopold Kohr, *The Overdeveloped Nations: The Diseconomies of Scale*, Schoken, NY, 1978.

John McMurtry, *Unequal Freedoms: The Global Market as an Ethical System*, Kumarian Press, Bloomfield, 1998.

John McMurtry, *Value Wars: The Global Market Versus the Life Economy*, Pluto Press, London, 2002.

Norman Myers & Jennifer Kent, *Perverse Subsidies: How Misused Tax Dollars Harm the Environment and the Economy*, Island Press, Washington DC, 2001.

Robert H. Nelson, *Economics as Religion: From Samuelson to Chicago and Beyond*, Penn State UP, PA, 2001.

James Robertson, *Transforming Economic Life*, Schumacher Briefing No. 1.

Guy Routh, *The Origins of Economic Ideas*, Macmillan Press, London, 1975.

Michael Rowbotham, *Goodbye America! Globalisation, Debt and the Dollar Empire*, Jon Carpenter Publishing, Oxford, 2000.

Michael Rowbotham, *The Grip of Death*, Jon Carpenter Publishing, Oxford, 1998.

E.F. Schumacher, *Small Is Beautiful: A Study Of Economics As If People Mattered*, Blond & Briggs Ltd, London, 1973.

Joseph Stiglitz, *Globalization and its Discontents*, Penguin, London, 2002.

Alan Twelvetrees (ed.), *Community Economic Development: Rhetoric or Reality?*, Community Development Foundation, London, 1998.

Other

Gary Alexander, *eGaia: Growing a Peaceful, Sustainable Earth Through Communications*, Lighthouse Books, 2002. See also: *http://sustainability.open.ac.uk/gary.*

William Blackstone (ed.). *Philiosophy and Environmental Crisis*, University of Georgia Press, Athens GA, 1974.

Rachel Carson, *Silent Spring*, Hamish Hamilton, London, 1963.

Noam Chomsky, *Media Control: The Spectacular Achievements of Propaganda (The Open Media Pamphlet Series, No. 1)*, Seven Stories Press, NY, 1997.

Theo Colborn, Diane Dumanoski & John Peterson Myers, *Our Stolen Future*, Plume, New York, 1996.

Richard Dawkins, *The Selfish Gene*, O.U.P., Oxford, 1976.

Oswaldo de Rivero, *The Myth of Development*, Zed Books, 2001, NY.

Pooran Desai & Sue Riddlestone, *Bioregional Solutions*, Schumacher Briefing No 8, p.27.

Peter Drucker, *The Practice of Management*, Heinemann, London, 1955.

John Dunn (ed.), *Democracy: The Unfinished Journey 508 BC to AD 1993*, OUP, Oxford, 1992.

Wayne Ellwood, *The No-Nonsense Guide to Globalisation*, Verso, London, 2002.

Paulo Freire, *Cultural Action for Freedom (Harvard Educational Review Monograph Series No. 1)*, Harvard Education Publishing Group, Cambridge MA, 1970.

Paulo Freire, *Pedagogy Of The Oppressed*, Continuum, NY, 1970.

Herbert Girardet, *Earthrise: How Can We Heal Our Injured Planet?*, Paladin Books, London, 1992.

David Held, *Democracy and the Global Order*, Polity Press, Cambridge, 1995.

David Held, Anthony McGrew, David Goldblatt & Jonathon Perraton, *Global Transformations: Politics, Economics and Culture*, Polity Press, Cambridge, 1999.

David Held (ed.), *A Globalizing World?: Culture, Economics, Politics (Understanding Social Change)*, Routledge, London, 2000.

Edward Herman & Noam Chomsky, *Manufacturing Consent: The Political Economy of the Mass Media*, Pantheon Books, NY, 1988.

Mae Wan Ho, *Genetic Engineering: Dream or Nightmare?*, Continuum, NY, 1998.

Robert Hutchison (ed.), *Ahead of Time—Birthday Letters to Mayer Hillman*, Policy Studies Institute, London, 2001.

Christopher Lasch, *The Revolt of the Elites*, Norton & Co, NY, 1995.

Jeremy Leggett, *The Carbon War: Global Warming and the End of the Oil Era*, Routledge, London, 2001.

Walter Lippman, *Public Opinion*, 1922.

James Lovelock, *Gaia: A New Look at Life on Earth*, OUP, Oxford, 1979.

John R. Macarthur, *Selling Free Trade: NAFTA, Washington and the Subversion of American Democracy*, Hill & Wang, NY, 2000.

George Monbiot, *Captive State*, Macmillan, London, 2000.

Helena Norberg-Hodge, Todd Merrifield & Steven Gorelick, *Bringing the Food Economy Home*, Kumarian Press, Bloomfield, 2002.

John Ralston-Saul, *Voltaire's Bastards: The Dictatorship of Reason in the West*, Penguin, Toronto, 1992.

Harvey Robbins & Michael Finley, *Why Change Doesn't Work: Why Initiatives Go Wrong and How to Try Again and Succeed*, Orion Business Books, London, 1997.

Ricardo Semler, *Maverick!*, Century, London, 1993.

George Soros, *On Globalisation*, PublicAffairs Ltd, NY, 2002, in *The New York Review of Books*, 23 May 2002.

Vandana Shiva, *Biopiracy: The Plunder of Nature and Knowledge*, South End Press, Cambridge MA.

Vandana Shiva, *Protect or Plunder*, Zed Books, London, 2001.

Vandana Shiva, *Stolen Harvest: The Hijacking of the Global Food Supply,* Southend Press, Cambridge MA, 1999.

Bob Sutcliffe, *100 Ways of Seeing an Unequal World*, Zed Books, NY, 2001.

Richard Swift, *The No-Nonsense Guide to Democracy*, Verso, London, 2002.

Luca Tacconi, *Biodiversity and Ecological Economics,* Earthscan, London, 2001.

Perry Walker, *We the People*, New Economics Foundation Notebook, London, 2002.

OTHER SCHUMACHER BRIEFINGS

The Schumacher Briefings are carefully researched, clearly written booklets on key aspects of sustainable development, published approximately twice a year. They offer readers:

• background information and an overview of the issue concerned
• an understanding of the state of play in the UK and elsewhere
• best practice examples of relevance for the issue under discussion
• an overview of policy implications and implementation.

No 1: Transforming Economic Life
A Millennial Challenge
James Robertson

Chapters include Transforming the System; A Common Pattern; Sharing the Value of Common Resources; Money and Finance; and The Global Economy. Published with the New Economics Foundation. **£5.00 pb**

No 2: Creating Sustainable Cities
Herbert Girardet

"An excellent brieifng"
—Scientific & Medical Network

Shows how cities can dramatically reduce their consumption of resources and energy, and at the same time greatly improve the quality of life of their citizens. Chapters include Urban Sustainability, Cities and their Ecological Footprint, The Metabolism of Cities, Prospects for Urban Farming, Smart Cities and Urban Best Practice. **£5.00 pb**

OTHER SCHUMACHER BRIEFINGS

No 3: The Ecology of Health
Robin Stott

Concerned with how environmental conditions affect the state of our health; how through new processes of participation we can regain control of what affects our health, and the kinds of policies that are needed to ensure good health for ourselves and our families. **£5.00 pb**

No 4: The Ecology of Money
Richard Douthwaite

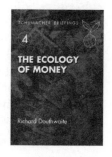

"This slim volume crams in a wide range of ideas about money"—Sustainable Economics

Explains why money has different effects according to its origins and purposes. Was it created to make profits for a commercial bank, or issued by government as a form of taxation? Or was it created by users themselves purely to facilitate their trade? This Briefing shows that it will be impossible to build a just and sustainable world until money creation is democratized. **£5.00 pb**

No 5: Contraction & Convergence
The Global Solution to Climate Change
Aubrey Meyer

"Hidden within this short book is a proposal which could and should alter the course of history."—The Ecologist

"A simple yet powerful concept that may yet break the deadlock of climate negotiations."—Red Pepper

The C&C framework, which has been pioneered and advocated by the Global Commons Institute at the United Nations over the past decade, is based on the thesis of 'Equity and Survival'. It seeks to ensure future prosperity and choice by applying the global rationale of precaution, equity and efficiency in that order. **£5.00 pb**

OTHER SCHUMACHER BRIEFINGS

No 6: Sustainable Education
Revisioning Learning & Change
Stephen Sterling

"A stimulating, challenging and thought-provoking book."—School Science Review

"A valuable contribution to the literature on education and sustainability."
—Environmental Education Research

Education is largely behind—rather than ahead of—other fields in developing new thinking and practice in response to the challenge of sustainability. The fundamental tasks are to • critique the prevailing educational and learning paradigm, which has become increasingly mechanistic and managerial • develop an ecologically informed education paradigm based on humanistic and sustainability values, systems thinking and the implications of complexity theory. An outline is given of a transformed education that can lead to transformative learning. **£5.00 pb**

No 7: The Roots of Health
Romy Fraser and Sandra Hill

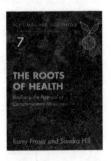

The advancements of modern medicine provide a sophisticated but mechanistic approach to health. Dazzled by its progress, we have lost touch with the simple remedies and body wisdom that were once a part of every household. By understanding the roots of health, we can begin to reclaim this wisdom, and to heal ourselves, our society and our environment. **£5.00 pb**

OTHER SCHUMACHER BRIEFINGS

No. 8: BioRegional Solutions
For Living on One Planet
Pooran Desai and Sue Riddlestone

"The entrepreneurial spirit of BioRegional has catalysed real and lasting examples of how we can meet our needs in a sustainable way and play fair with the developing world. This is the new mainstream, not an alternative lifestyle."— Anita Roddick

"Some people talk about sustainable development—others just get out there and do it! BioRegional does just that, coming up with inspiring but practical initiatives that address climate change, waste reduction and the all-important challenge of regenerating local communities and economies sustainably." —Jonathon Porritt, Programme Director, Forum for the Future, Chairman, UK Sustainable Development Commission

We live in a consumer society, and over-consumption is the driving force of environmental degradation. This stark reality led Pooran Desai and Sue Riddlestone to found BioRegional Development Group. In this Briefing they show how we can meet more of our needs for wood products, paper, textiles, food and housing from local renewable and waste resources. They outline the theoretical framework of bioregional development and the award-winning practical solutions that BioRegional have developed with industry partners. They quantify how we can significantly reduce CO2 emissions and recycle waste, and so greatly reduce our ecological footprint. **£6.00 pb**

Schumacher Briefings are available from The Schumacher Society (details on following page). All bookshop orders and foreign rights enquiries should be sent to Green Books (details on back cover).

THE SCHUMACHER SOCIETY
Promoting Human-Scale Sustainable Development

The Society was founded in 1978 after the death of economist and philosopher E.F. Schumacher, author of seminal books such as *Small is Beautiful, Good Work* and *A Guide for the Perplexed*. He sought to explain that the gigantism of modern economic and technological systems diminishes the well-being of individuals and communities, and the health of nature. His work has significantly influenced the thinking of our time.

The aims of the Schumacher Society are to:

- Help assure that ecological issues are approached, and solutions devised, as if people matter, emphasising appropriate scale in human affairs;

- Emphasise that humanity can't do things in isolation. Long-term thinking and action, and connectedness to other life forms, are crucial;

- Stress holistic values, and the importance of a profound understanding of the subtle human qualities that transcend our material existence.

At the heart of the Society's work are the Schumacher Lectures, held in Bristol every year since 1978, and now also in other major cities in the UK. Our distinguished speakers, from all over the world, have included Amory Lovins, Herman Daly, Jonathon Porrit, James Lovelock, Wangari Maathai, Matthew Fox, Ivan Illich, Fritjof Capra, Arne Naess, Maneka Gandhi, James Robertson, Vandana Shiva and Zac Goldsmith.

Tangible expressions of our efforts over the last 25 years are: the Schumacher Lectures; the Schumacher Briefings; Green Books publishing house; Schumacher College at Dartington, and the Small School at Hartland, Devon. The Society, a non-profit making company, is based in Bristol and London. We receive charitable donations through the Environmental Research Association in Hartland, Devon.

Schumacher UK Members receive Schumacher Briefings, Schumacher Newsletters, discounts on tickets to Schumacher Lectures & Events and a range of discounts from other organisations within the Schumacher Circle, including Schumacher College, Resurgence Magazine and the Centre for Alternative Technology (CAT).

**The Schumacher Society, CREATE Environment Centre,
Smeaton Road, Bristol BS1 6XN Tel/Fax: 0117 903 1081
admin@schumacher.org.uk www.schumacher.org.uk**